D0920945

The Innovator's Field Guide

Accelerators for Entrepreneurs, Innovators, and Change Agents

Jeff D. Standridge

Fitting Words
Hendersonville, Tennessee

Fitting Words
105 Hazel Path
Hendersonville, Tennessee 37075
www.fittingwords.net

Library of Congress Cataloging-in-Publication Data
Standridge, Jeff D.

ISBN 978-0-9979136-4-4

Printed in the United States of America

1 2 3 4 5 6 7 8 9 10

CONTENTS

YOU ARE GO FOR LAUNCH!

Innovation in any setting can be daunting. Being an entrepreneur is gut-wrenching, and filling the role of change agent takes a level of energy that most do not feel they possess. When you have the responsibility of being a change agent in your business, organization, or community, the burden of leadership weighs heavily on your shoulders. I've been in all three positions and have the battle scars to prove it.

Creating something new or improving a pre-existing process has always been my approach to work and to life. I've always tinkered and tweaked until the process is running on greased grooves. Being an innovator has its own set of challenges. Demands on your time, expectations of always being able to "create," and constantly being presented with problems that require emotional and physical effort to solve only represent a subatomic particle of the stressors chained to innovation.

My love of "making things better" led to a reputation as an innovator and change agent early in my career. Back then, my research interests focused on identifying the differentiators of success between the top performers and average performers within an organization. Taking this data, I created "success models" that could be used to select, coach, develop, and train top performers. The business world lured me into the fold *because* of my reputation as an innovator and change agent. Those monikers have afforded me the opportunity to perfect these approaches across five continents and with countless clients. That status has also carried me throughout multiple companies, boards, organizations, and communities. It's an energizing role to play for sure, but I know all too well that it can also be immensely stressful.

If that wasn't enough to fill one's mind, the pressure of being an entrepreneur takes up the rest of your mental capacity. Entrepreneurs innovate while simultaneously being change agents. If wearing those hats isn't stressful enough, payrolls and payables have to be met. Entrepreneurs must make certain their customers are served, their employees are paid, and their bills are current, while also ensuring life needs are met. No matter what blows up at work, the kids still must be housed, shuttled to school, fed, clothed, and put to bed.

Enduring the life of an innovator, entrepreneur, and/or change agent takes the strength of Hercules, the wisdom of Solomon, and the endurance of Jim Fixx. The purpose of *The Innovator's Field Guide* is to provide you with respite, inspiration, and hope during those times when everything appears bleak.

You're likely familiar with the concept of an *accelerator*. In most cases, an accelerator is an extended program, usually twelve to sixteen weeks in length, that is designed to help early-stage entrepreneurs fast-track their ventures. The process helps entrepreneurs find and traverse the critical paths to gain traction and, ultimately, success within their chosen markets. I've taken the opportunity to adapt the accelerator concept for use in large and small companies, educational institutions, non-profits, and other organizations. Remolding the paradigm enables organizations to find, extract, and operationalize innovations from within the ranks of their current teams. I now spend a considerable amount of my time working with those types of organizations.

In my coaching and consulting practice, I annually conduct over 400 individual engagements with innovators, entrepreneurs, and change agents. I have recognized the similarities in their functions and the strenuous emotional demands they face. *The Innovator's Field Guide* is designed to address many of those demands by allowing readers to step away from the fray. Use this guide to take a few moments of respite and to reflect on specific aspects of your role. By no means is using this guide meant to be additional work—you have enough already. The stories and concepts contained within are designed to be a "breather" for you that will spur you on to fresh, immediately applicable insights.

The best use of *The Innovator's Field Guide* is to take a set time each week *to stop* what you're doing and to *engage* with one of the accelerators. Read the material, reflect on the questions and actions, and then go back to work. Over the next day or two, think about those questions and actions. When you are ready, take a few more moments to sit down and do what leaders do—answer the questions, plan the necessary activities, and then *take action*! I guarantee you'll be glad you did.

When you're ready, I'd love to hear about the impact. Give me a shout. It would be an honor to speak with you.

A FUTURE ORIENTATION

"The world makes way for the man who knows where he's going."

Ralph Waldo Emerson

I've repeatedly seen it—successful people have a future orientation. They may not know exactly how they're going to get there, but they have a crystal-clear vision of their intended destination. Underlying this vision, storming towards the uber-successful is a three-step framework involving Clarity, Focus, and Execution.

I first learned the power of this trinity by accident. I worked my way through college as an emergency medical technician for a hospital-based ambulance service. I decided to major in respiratory therapy for one simple reason—I wanted to be a member of the flight team aboard Angel One at Arkansas Children's Hospital. The day I began the professional portion of the respiratory therapy program, I waltzed into the department director at Arkansas Children's Hospital and declared, "I just began respiratory-therapy school, and when I graduate, I'm going to come here and fly on your helicopter. So, if you'd like to hire me—know you can train me during the next few months, so I'll be ready when I graduate."

I didn't get the job that day. A few months later, after observing me during a clinical rotation, that department director hired me. The day after I graduated, I was a member of the Angel One Flight Team. I spent the next several years living my dream. Fate had another surprise in store for me: another member of that team was my future wife, Lori.

Successful people have *clarity* on where they are going. They develop a relentless *focus* on that destination, and they understand how to impeccably *execute* that plan. Those three keys can make the difference between where you are and where you want to be. Make it happen!

A FUTURE ORIENTATION

ACCELERATORS

 What does your ideal future look like in three, five, and/or ten years? Spend the time necessary to develop crystal clarity on that desired future.

 On what things must you intently focus to fulfill that vision or to arrive at that desired destination?

 What things must you achieve or accomplish in the next twelve months to take you as far as possible toward that vision or destination?

 What key actions must you take daily or weekly in order to achieve or accomplish those twelve-month milestones?

IN THE MARKET FOR SOME SNAKE OIL?

"I know half the money I spend on advertising is wasted, but I can never find out which half."

John Wanamaker

Exactly thirty-seven seconds after an entrepreneur opens a business, solicitations from those representing fuzzy business disciplines—SEO (search engine optimization), social media marketing, online brand consulting, and the like—all of whom attach guru or maven after the discipline name—start rolling in. For every single reputable company that can and will raise your visibility to potential customers, there are fifty companies that will sell you digital-marketing snake oil. There is no such thing as a "surefire" online marketing campaign or "special mojo" that will rocket your company's website to the top of a search engine's category results. In coaching my business clients, I tell them that there is no such thing as a bad marketing medium, as long as it puts you in front of your target audience and it generates a measurable return on your investment (ROI).

Irreputable companies bank on the difficulties in results-tracking to sell you their services—hence the reference to "fuzzy" business disciplines. Marketing, in any form, is a necessary part of your business's success, but how do you separate the wheat from the chaff? One might think of marketing in terms of a baseball player's at-bat statistics. Even the Babe Ruths of the marketing world are going to strike out occasionally, but their overall percentage of hits is the metric that matters.

When approached by any marketing company, ask how they will measure success. Inquire about the ROI for purchasing their services. Marketing is an investment of capital, and you expect a return above what you invest. Should a marketing service either not understand the concept of ROI or not be able to give you an idea of what results their previous clients realized with their services—walk away. The success of your business is not measured by an increase of hits, followers, or likes. You're in business to make money. If a marketer doesn't know how to translate those hits, followers, or likes into dollar signs … find someone who can. Trust me; they're out there.

IN THE MARKET FOR SOME SNAKE OIL?

ACCELERATORS

 Take a quick inventory of your marketing spending. How much do you presently spend, and in what categories do you spend it (print advertising, SEO, digital ads, pay-per-click, etc.)?

 Now identify the actual measurable marketing spending. How much money do you spend on marketing activities for which *you know* the return on those investments?

 Examine those other dollars (where you don't know the return) and consider how you might better spend them to get a measurable return.

GAINING WISDOM

"A single conversation with a wise man is better than ten years of study."

Chinese Proverb

Alexander Pope said, "A little learning is a dangerous thing." Sandy knew that phrase when she began her teaching career, but didn't understand the full impact of the statement. Her head was filled with pedagogical theory and a working knowledge of her subject matter—history.

Sandy plunged in with an ambitious lesson plan, bringing her love of literature to the history lectures that were carefully typed and ready for delivery. When the students received the syllabus, many expressed shock when they saw that she had assigned various literary readings to supplement their history texts. Sandy left the classroom after that first day feeling confident and extremely pleased with herself.

The next morning, Sandy found a note in her mailbox. The headmaster of the school wanted to see Sandy ASAP. The headmaster didn't ask Sandy to sit down when he began. "Mr. Sizemore, the high school's English teacher, wants to know why you're assigning your students many of the same books that he is having them read."

The headmaster went on to explain that Mr. Sizemore, a thirty-year school veteran, and master teacher, had constructed an award-winning curriculum around carefully chosen works. Sizemore was naturally curious why this newcomer was entering his domain. Sandy was embarrassed that she didn't reach out to her fellow teachers. She didn't consider that while everyone taught in individual classrooms, the faculty was still a team.

Before you think you know it all, consult with those who might actually know it all. Successful innovators, entrepreneurs, and change agents leverage a large network of mentors to broaden their base of expertise. The wisdom you can gather from those around you is an invaluable tool, and you don't always have to reinvent the wheel.

GAINING WISDOM
ACCELERATORS

 List the areas of expertise that you don't currently have, but need, to be optimally successful.

 Identify the experts to whom you have access (or can get access through others) who can help fill the gaps in your expertise.

 Prioritize the knowledge and guidance you need now, and make a plan to get it from the ones who have it.

CHANGE THE WORLD,
ONE IDEA AT A TIME

"I like to say that the one thing that all people who succeed in changing the world have in common is that they at least tried."

Kevin Systrom

The fourth employee hired by a company is rarely the person recognized for having a world-changing idea. The headlines are rife with a successful company's founder. For example, we know IKEA was started by Ingvar Kamprad. The brand revolutionized home furnishings by selling flat-pack, or assemble-it-yourself, furniture. There are anecdotes galore about the man, now known as one of the world's richest people. One of the most memorable is Ingvar's father complaining about his being a late riser, so Ingvar set an alarm clock and removed the "off" button. He's also famously cheap and commonly stays in affordable hotels when traveling. One anecdote you won't hear much about Ingvar Kamprad is the day he had the epiphany for flat-pack furniture. That story is IKEA's fourth employee, Gillis Lundgren's, to tell.

When Lundgren started at IKEA, the company sold mail-order, fully assembled furnishings. One night in 1956, Lundgren bought a new table. Try as he may, Lundgren could not get the table to fit in his car. There was no other way to get his new acquisition home short of taking the legs off, so out came a saw. As the sawdust piled around Lundgren's feet, he undoubtedly considered how he was going to reassemble the table when he returned home. That's when it hit him. What if IKEA designed and sold furniture that the consumer assembled at home? IKEA's shipping and production costs would plummet, and no one would ever be faced with sawing off table legs ever again. Ingvar Kamprad loved the idea and today, you can't throw a tennis ball in a Walmart or Costco without hitting a piece of flat-packed furniture.

It doesn't matter if you're the fourth, or ninety-fourth, employee hired by a company. You can still change the world by implementing better ways of doing what you already do.

CHANGE THE WORLD,
ONE IDEA AT A TIME
ACCELERATORS

 How much better would your business, organization, or work area be if everyone came up with one *massive* improvement to the way you currently do things?

 Get your team on board by holding a contest for the top one, three, or five idea(s) for making massive improvements to the work you already do. Establish a prize and let everyone on the team vote for the winner(s).

 Once you have the top improvements identified, launch an implementation team for each improvement and appoint the winner as the Team Leader.

MEET THEM ON THEIR TURF

"At Netflix, we think you have to build a sense of responsibility where people care about the enterprise. Hard work, like long hours at the office, doesn't matter as much to us. We care about great work."

Reed Hastings

Civil servants are some of the most underappreciated members of our society. John, a decorated Vietnam veteran who had been a rural county's Veterans Affairs Officer for the past twenty-five years, was widely considered one of the most impactful officers in his state. He was asked what the secret was to his success.

He grinned and said, "It's no secret. I don't keep office hours."

When pressed on this confounding statement, John nodded, saying, "Oh, I do the paperwork. I work the phones. In fact, for the first two years on this job, I barely left the office. And you know what? Very few veterans came to see me for help. I could not understand why they wouldn't. They knew where I was. Many of them knew me personally. But they didn't come."

"After I had realized that they weren't coming to me, I had to find them," he explained. "They have gone to the ends of the earth for our country. The least I could do was show them enough respect to go the short distance to where they are."

John got out of the office and went to where the veterans were. He went to VFW halls. He met veterans in their workplaces. He went to their functions, meetings, churches, and homes. Recently returned from duty, veterans had lives they had put on hold and were anxious to pick up where they had left off. They didn't have extra time to spend driving to the Veterans Affairs office to wait for their number to be called.

There's more to a business than simply opening your doors and hanging up a sign; sometimes you need to meet your clients where they are. If you're an entrepreneur or salesperson and you want to double your sales, try doubling the amount of time you spend face to face with qualified prospects and customers. Now that's a thought …

MEET THEM ON THEIR TURF
ACCELERATORS

✗ How many hours a week (on average) do you spend actually interacting with qualified prospects, customers, or key stakeholders?

✗ What are the things that distract or prevent you from spending more time with your customers or stakeholders?

✗ Put a plan in place to address these distractions and make a commitment to double the amount of time you are engaged with customers or stakeholders.

DON'T JUST DO
SOMETHING—SIT THERE!

"The ultimate value of life depends upon awareness and the power of contemplation rather than upon mere survival."

Aristotle

Scotland's King Robert the Bruce had a problem. He had ascended the throne in 1306 to a fragmented kingdom. Many Scots did not recognize the Bruce as their liege, and other factions vied for control of the Scottish throne. To add to the new king's woes, the English had also laid claim to Scotland, and England's armies held strategic points throughout the country. Three months after his coronation, the Bruce and his army were ambushed by the English at two key battles that resulted in three of Robert's four brothers, as well as his sister, being executed. Legend has it that Robert the Bruce fled the battlefield and took refuge in a nearby cave to escape capture.

His family, army, and country broken, the Bruce surely thought his life couldn't get much worse and considered leaving Scotland behind. Sitting at the cave's entrance, the king saw a spider weaving an intricate web. The Bruce had nothing better to do and watched the spider for hours. At one point, the spider tried to connect two far-apart strands. Six times the spider tried to leap the gap and six times he failed. Finally, on the seventh try, the spider made the jump and connected the loose ends. The King of Scotland thought that if a tiny spider wouldn't give up, neither would he. Robert the Bruce went on to unite his kingdom and defeat the English eight years later at the Battle of Bannockburn.

The story of Robert the Bruce may be a simple legend, but it illustrates more than perseverance. When we don't succeed, we must be receptive to seeing "failure" from a different point of view. Had Robert the Bruce stomped that spider out of anger over his situation and not observed the creature's lesson, the history of Scotland would be quite different. While some people advocate the adage, "Don't *just sit* there—do something," often the best adaptation of that adage is, "Don't *just do* something—sit there."

DON'T JUST DO
SOMETHING—SIT THERE!
ACCELERATORS

 In what areas of your work or business are you prone to "give up" prematurely?

 What areas of your work or business are perplexing you right now? Spend some time some time contemplating those areas.

 What three actions can you take today to move the ball forward in your work or business?

FREEDOM FROM CONSTRAINTS

"Nighttime is when I brainstorm; last thing, when the family's asleep and I'm alone, I think about the next day's writing and plan a strategy for my assault on the blank page."

Athol Fugard

An adage used in college economics classes is, "economics is driving a car looking in the rearview mirror," meaning that business analysis is heavily weighted by historical data. There is undoubtedly merit in examining past performance; however, being shackled by bar charts on PowerPoints seldom produces an original thought. Inspiration comes when we consider what is possible in the future, not how we did in the past.

Turn off your monitor and put the reports away. Take a blank sheet of paper from your desk and do some old-school brainstorming. Create an all-out assault on the blank page. Write down single words that apply to your current problem, innovation, or project. Don't think about what you can do—write down what you would do without having to justify expenses or man-hours. Spend no more than five or ten minutes on this portion of the exercise. After you've exhausted those single words, go back and review the list detailing why those words were present. For example, if you wrote down "long term," define what time parameters the project entails.

You've just created a dream on paper free of historical data or preconceived notions about what is "possible." Those possibilities may never happen in the manner you've envisioned, but you've started a process that asks, "Why not?" or "How can I?" One might think of this as the stone a sculptor starts with before chipping away to release a statue's true form. If you begin any thought process with the cannots and should nots, you limit your imagination and creativity. Only when those two elements are unleashed can true innovations happen.

FREEDOM FROM CONSTRAINTS
ACCELERATORS

 About your business, your current project, innovation, or business problem, complete this question: "Wouldn't it be great if … ?"

 What three things might you do this week to enable this vision to become a reality?

 What three things might you do consistently and repeatedly to bring this vision to reality over the coming days, weeks, or months?

POWERED BY TEAMWORK

"Building product is not about having a large team to manage. It is about having a small team with the right people on it."

Fred Wilson

Fact: a true iconoclast is unicorn rare. Popular culture has sold us on the idea that innovators dig within their souls and against all the odds come up with the solution to save the day—all alone. The pictures history paints of the Thomas Edisons and Henry Fords is that they did everything from unclogging toilets to making accounts receivable calls on top of being innovators. What would Jeff Bezos be doing right now if the thousands of Sues and Bills stopped pulling orders in his warehouses? Bezos wouldn't be rolling himself in the glory of imagining and implementing new programs for Amazon; he would be wondering why his team fell apart.

The true success of any innovator is not limited to his or her invention or idea, but the often-forgotten success lies in how that person created and maintained their team. The symbiotic relationship between "the idea" and those that make the idea a reality can never be dismissed. One might think of this as the old Reese's Peanut Butter Cup commercials where a bar of chocolate ends up in a jar of peanut butter followed by the tagline, "Two great tastes that taste great together."

As you develop your confidence and skills as an innovator or change agent, remember that team-building is critical to your success. The more genuine you are with your vision, the more infectious it will become for your team. Your goal is to empower your team to make good creative decisions, as well as being committed to your vision at the same level of passion you are. If you can do all of that, you will be amazed at the platform effect your team will produce.

POWERED BY TEAMWORK
ACCELERATORS

 Find at least two mentors who will give you feedback about your leadership strengths and your blind spots.

 Identify the top three most critical tasks or areas of responsibility in your business or team for which you are not the ideal person to carry them out.

 Develop a plan to get those tasks or areas of responsibility completed by someone who's skilled and/or naturally gifted in those areas.

9

INSPIRATION LIES ALL AROUND YOU

"I get inspiration from my everyday life."

Hayao Miyazaki

Jack Ma, the founder of Alibaba, is no stranger to rejection. China's richest man wasn't the greatest student. He scored a whopping 1 on a 120-point college entrance math exam and was rejected by Harvard 10 times. Ma settled on majoring in English at the appropriately named Hangzhou Normal University. After getting his degree, Ma applied for thirty jobs and received thirty rejection letters. Prospects were so thin that Ma interviewed to work in the kitchen at a Kentucky Fried Chicken. Twenty-four others applied at KFC with Ma and twenty-three got jobs. Jack Ma was not one of the "lucky ones." The only work Ma could find was a twelve-dollar-a-month gig teaching English.

Even when Ma had the idea of using the Internet to connect Chinese businesses with the rest of the world, Alibaba was something of a flop. The industrial-sized eBay didn't show a profit for its first three years and was eighteen months away from bankruptcy. Now Alibaba is worth about $250 billion. Why? Jack Ma credits a portion of his success to Forrest Gump.

As ludicrous as it sounds, the film version of Forrest Gump's simplistic "box of chocolate" witticisms gave Jack hope to remain persistent in his vision. The lesson here is not persistence—that's the common denominator in examining any visionary's success. The lesson is to draw inspiration anywhere you find it. Remove the blinders and look around! If you are always seeking out gurus living on mountaintops for guidance, you're missing out on messages that are in your world every day. From a line of a cheesy pop song to a word of encouragement from your usually annoying neighbor, inspiration can be all around you. Are you ready to listen?

INSPIRATION LIES ALL AROUND YOU

ACCELERATORS

 About three weeks ago, you identified areas within your work or business where you are prone to "give up" prematurely. What actions have you taken in the past three weeks or so to display common persistence in those areas? Do you need to renew your commitment in this regard?

 Look back over your life and career. Where have you experienced temporary setbacks, yet reigned triumphant in the end? What inspired you to keep going? From where did this inspiration come?

 From where do you normally derive inspiration today?

 In what areas of your work or business do you need inspiration now?

CHALLENGE YOUR UNDERLYING ASSUMPTIONS

"When businesses go through hard times, through down markets, what they do is they challenge every basic assumption of how they operate. They innovate. They create disruption for a while that leads them to even greater heights when the economy turns around."

Jeb Bush

No book about inspiration would be complete without a few quotes from humanity's smartest individual, Albert Einstein. You've probably heard, or seen social-media memes with these quotes from Einstein:

N "Not everything that counts can be counted."

N "The definition of insanity is doing the same thing over and over again and expecting different results."

✓ "Everyone is a genius. But if you judge a fish by its ability to climb a tree, it will live its whole life believing that it is stupid."

The problem is, Albert Einstein never said any of those things. We believe Einstein was the originator of those encouraging words because we've read social-media posts or "just know" Einstein said all those things. Don't take my word for it; do your own legwork to ferret out the truth behind Einstein's misquotations.

Misattribution of quotations is an example of deceptive thinking—or, put another way, the difference between our perception and the truth. Individuals and organizations can explain away all sorts of ills. "We're keeping it between the ditches." "It's the best we can do." "It will work itself out in the wash." How often have we heard or used those phrases as an avoidance mechanism?

To be a successful leader, our premises should be periodi-cally reexamined, and our points of deceptive thinking should be confronted if we are to grow ourselves and our teams. If you don't think you're susceptible to deceptive thinking, how did you react to the Einstein quotes if you believed he said them? Was your first thought to research if that was correct or, were you flustered, safe in the belief Einstein said those pithy lines?

CHALLENGE YOUR UNDERLYING ASSUMPTIONS

ACCELERATORS

What facts or assumptions do you need to challenge in your business, project, or company?

How might you go about validating (or invalidating) those assumptions?

Where are you prone to fall prey to your own "deceptive thinking?"

FAILURE IS THE BREAKFAST
OF CHAMPIONS

"Failure should be our teacher, not our undertaker. Failure is delay, not defeat. It is a temporary detour, not a dead end. Failure is something we can avoid only by saying nothing, doing nothing, and being nothing."

Denis Waitley

The "F" word is whispered in cubicles and at water coolers. When it becomes public knowledge, the office's gossip switchboard lights up like a dysfunctional Christmas tree. No one speaks directly of it, but the stigma-laden innuendo will always be remembered. Just one mistake, and the aggrieved party will always be branded with the scarlet letter "F" for failure. When you or a compatriot misses the mark, does the associated shame feel like that? If so, both your workplace culture and personal perception need an adjustment.

The pressure to achieve a result other than 100% success is so engrained in business that it's easy to forget that an open and honest analysis of not achieving a goal is more important than studying success. The tendency to mitigate or simply not discuss suboptimal results can be damaging to your team. Because when we hide the elements of "what didn't work," we're laying the groundwork for others to fall into the same traps.

We can change the perception of "failure" in incremental steps. Often the missteps of the past cannot be rectified, but we can influence the future by learning from our mistakes. The first step would be to ask yourself or your team member about one thing they would have done differently to have changed a suboptimal outcome. Then, we hold ourselves or our team accountable to implement that change—not for the initial "failure" itself. The goal is not to create an environment that excuses not achieving results. The goal is to foster a culture that promotes growth. Remember, for the uber-successful, there's no such thing as failure, only feedback. It only becomes a failure when you quit!

FAILURE IS THE BREAKFAST OF CHAMPIONS

ACCELERATORS

 List the top three most significant failures you've ever experienced.

 What themes can you find in those failures? How might you address them for future success?

 Where are you experiencing feedback (disguised as failure) in your business today?

ACHIEVE AND CELEBRATE, REPEAT

"When eating an elephant, take one bite at a time."

Creighton Abrams

The ad tagline "I'm going to Disneyland!" has tainted Americans' view of success. Seeing sports stars winning the big game and exclaiming they're headed for a well-deserved vacation has planted a destructive seed, that seed being the idea that we only are successful when we reach the pinnacle of our craft. This mentality disregards the thousands of successes that had to be chained together that allowed the athlete to win the big game. The hours of practice, making the varsity team in high school, bring drafted, and any other milestones along the way were successes, but we latch on to the big win as being that person's only success.

If we only celebrate or recognize completion of end goals, we're doing ourselves and our team members a disservice.

In not recognizing the milestones that culminate in the completion of a larger goal, our team members may become discouraged. Our team members might not recognize their contributions to the bigger picture, and their performance can drop off, believing their work doesn't matter. This is a situation that no leader wants, as that mindset is infectious to other team members.

As you set the standards for any given project, create rewards for plateaus that both motivate and celebrate the individual victories. The spirit of competitiveness can also be invoked by giving higher rewards or praise to individuals who come in with quality work under time and under budgets. It's up to you as a leader to craft celebratory victory laps for project plateaus. In doing so, the scope of projects will feel smaller, and your team will be more motivated with shorter goals in sight. Remember, the only way to eat an elephant is one bite at a time.

ACHIEVE AND CELEBRATE, REPEAT

ACCELERATORS

 What "elephants" do you have in your business right now that need to be broken down into bite-sized projects?

 Where and how can you use this "Project Plateau" euphemism to create short successes?

 What process can you establish so that you, your leaders, and your teammates adopt the habit of creating and celebrating short-term milestones that are tied to longer-term success?

EXIT INCREMENTAL,
ENTER EXPONENTIAL

"An exponential growth is a simple doubling. One becomes
two becomes four."

Peter Diamandis

To be an innovator, one does not always have to create a
brand spanking new process or widget. Some innovations are
a change in the way we approach the commonplace. A few
years back Arizona State University (ASU) started the arduous
plan for renovating Sun Devil Stadium. One can imagine the
laundry list of upgrades one would want to incorporate in a
reimagined sports stadium. However, better flow to the food
vendors and bathroom access would not be what one would
consider an innovation. Wishing the stadium to be something
unique, ASU solicited the advice of some of their top alumni.

Enter Jack Furst, the founder of the private equity firm
Oak Stream Investors. After graduating from ASU in 1981,

Jack worked on Wall Street before striking out on his own. What separates Furst from his peers is a vision that includes a strong bond to the community. When ASU asked for his opinions on the stadium's renovations, they got more than they bargained for.

In Jack's mind, a facility that was utilized for only football games and the odd concert did not fulfill the stadium's potential. Furst's vision was to make Sun Devil Stadium into a place that would function as a community hub, open daily to the public—food vendors, outdoor movies, festivals, or any other activity that would make Sun Devil Stadium an integral part of the Tempe/Phoenix community in the coming years. From a financial perspective, turning a capital investment from a two percent to potentially a hundred percent utilization rate is staggering. This is referred to as exponential or "10x" thinking.

When we marry our core values with the opportunities life presents us, unexpected innovations can crop up in the most unlikely of places and transform life as we know it.

EXIT INCREMENTAL,
ENTER EXPONENTIAL
ACCELERATORS

 Quickly list ten ways that you could exponentially transform your business, company, team, or project. (Think ten times growth or transformation.)

 Select two or three of those ten ways that seem to be most feasible.

 Engage in a conversation with members of your team about how to bring these transformations to reality.

EMPATHETIC DESIGN

"The main tenet of design thinking is empathy for the people you're trying to design for. Leadership is exactly the same thing—building empathy for the people that you're entrusted to help."

David M. Kelley

An insurance provider that caters to senior citizens was revamping its identification-card system. The thirty-something who oversaw the technical aspects of the project presented a new software system that integrated ordering physical cards with electronic card maintenance on a new smartphone app. Amidst the talk of efficiencies and cost savings, a customer service representative noticed that a function to order multiple physical cards had been dropped from the new software. When questioned, the project manager didn't understand why anyone would want multiple physical cards. The customer service representative explained that many of their policyholders had multiple caregivers who rotated taking the policyholders to the doctor's appointments. Multiple cards were ordered for emergency situations or as a convenience for each caregiver. The lack of a quantity order function would create inefficiencies for frontline staff and customers alike.

The project manager incredulously replied that "I'd just use the app," and quashed bringing back the feature. Many seniors are wary of technology, and giving caregivers passwords to accounts that contain financial information is not always a safe alternative. While the new integrated card system was implemented per specifications, was the project manager successful? One could argue that in the efficient execution of her task, she had met her goal. However, the project manager was not guided by either the company's core values or customer's needs. In that respect, and certainly in my mind, the project manager underachieved. Empathetic design considers the users and customers and builds their natural inclinations, wishes, and desires into the design of the product or service.

How often do we lose touch with our end users or customers in a rush to achieve our goals? The next time you have a project, work backward from the end user's perspective. Begin by asking, "How can this project or innovation enhance our customer's experience?" and then merge your project's goals with those answers. With the customers' interests at heart, there's really no way to lose.

EMPATHETIC DESIGN
ACCELERATORS

⚡ What assumptions have you made about your customers' or stakeholders' needs, wants, or natural inclinations?

⚡ How might you go about validating or invalidating those assumptions? (Research the terms "Customer Discovery" or "Talking to Humans" for some ideas in this regard.)

⚡ In what three areas might the process of "Customer Discovery" help you right now?

⚡ Create a process and an action plan to test these three most significant assumptions under which you, your business, and/or your team have been operating.

TO BUILD STRONG TEAMS, BUILD STRONG TEAMMATES

"Building a great team is the lifeblood of any startup, and finding great talent is one of the hardest and costliest tasks any CEO will ever face."

Jay Samit

"Turnover costs are too high; we have to retain our employees!" shouted HR.

"If he can't do the job, get rid of him and find someone who will!" shouted the executives, even more loudly.

The paradox of reducing voluntary attrition while holding a disposable workforce mentality catches many of us in a precarious position. Time and budgetary constraints never allow for enough training or development, and it's tempting to use the sink-or-swim method of developing team members. When a new associate is struggling but was promising enough to be selected for your team, we have two options. We can plug someone else in the slot and hope for the best, or we can coach and develop that team member to help them reach their potential. As leaders, we have an obligation to provide our team members with the necessary tools for success.

If we think someone is too broken for their job duties, consider a little-known art form from Japan. Around the 15th century, the Japanese began mending cracked and shattered pottery in an exceptional fashion. The process is called *kintsugi*, which translates to "golden joinery." The artisan infuses the cracks and tears with a lacquer laced with a precious metal—most often gold. At the end of the process, the vessel is both useful and a unique work of art. The philosophical motive behind *kintsugi* is that breakage and subsequent repair should not be disguised, but should tell the history of the object.

How different would our organizations be if we practiced *kintsugi* on our associates as the first option? How many hours is it worth trying to mend your broken vessels? Is the loss of output, interviewing, advertising costs, and disruption of team dynamics is worth a few hours of extra training? Turnover costs are difficult to fully pin down, but spending an hour or two each week with an underperforming team member is much cheaper than starting from scratch.

The Innovator's Field Guide

TO BUILD STRONG TEAMS, BUILD STRONG TEAMMATES
ACCELERATORS

 List three areas of underperformance on your team or in your business right now.

 What are the common themes of the three areas of underperformance?

 How can you practice *kintsugi* to transform the situation in your business?

CREATING FORWARD MOMENTUM

"Trust your gut feeling about things, listen to what others are saying, and look at the results of your actions. Once you know the truth, you can set about taking action to improve. Everyone will be better for it."

Jack Canfield

Coffeehouses throughout America are filled with people throwing out great idea after world-changing plans, so why are people sipping on lattes instead of making them happen? Many people seem to have bought fully into the notion that success is just "one idea away." If someone would just buy into that idea, fame and riches would follow. To an extent, "one idea away from success" is valid. However, simply having the idea is only a portion of the equation necessary for success. Ideas must be implemented. Should we not have the skill set or impetus to move thought to action, one's chances for success are grim. I've heard it said that "It's not enough to stare up the steps. One must also step up the stairs." And so it is with our ideas.

Having an idea is the easy part. A brainstorming session can create a dozen brilliant ideas that we can get all giddy over. Until we take one step, just one step breathing life into that idea, it's a useless exercise. That one step can be a baby step, but it must be designed to create forward momentum. Let's say you have an idea for a website and you're in the daydreaming stages. Go ahead and buy the domain name before you plan anything else. In many cases, you're looking at a twenty-dollar investment, but it's a symbolic step. You now own the vehicle to make your website a reality. The next small step could be creating content or designing a logo.

Timetables aren't as important as building forward momentum. If you're familiar with the "Compound Effect," you know that *seemingly small actions, consistently applied, over time, yield MASSIVE results.* Whatever helps you move forward, even as tiny as those seemingly small actions are, will eventually build on each other. You'll likely find that momentum is not a linear, but an exponential expression of growth. Small successes build an excitement that you will be unable to contain. That enthusiasm will become infectious as you have tangible wins to show to others. Then there will be no stopping you.

CREATING FORWARD
MOMENTUM
ACCELERATORS

 What three ideas have you been dreaming of yet waiting to implement?

 Which of these three would produce the greatest results for you if they were implemented quickly?

 For that one, most important idea, what "seemingly small action," could you take right now to create forward momentum? Take that action!

SMELLING THE ROSES

"Give yourself a gift of five minutes of contemplation in awe of everything you see around you. Go outside and turn your attention to the many miracles around you. This five-minutes-a-day regimen of appreciation and gratitude will help you focus your life in awe."

Wayne Dyer

The Appalachian Trail spans 2,175 miles from Georgia to Maine. Every year approximately 2,000 people attempt to hike the five-million-step trek, with a quarter of those backpackers completing the trail. How long do you think you would last if you counted every step just looking straight down at the trail? Never looking up at the scenery or wildlife, head down and ears back walking and counting. A day? A week? The net result is you would never make it to the end of the trail.

How often do we treat the day-to-day grind like a joyless walk on the Appalachian Trail? Getting to the office in the morning kicks it all off. You're stuck in traffic, and the car next to you is thumping an indecipherable bass beat. What joy is there in a whump-whump that more closely resembles a migraine than any music you'd listen to? The joy could be looking over at that driver and seeing how much those alien beats uplift them. That person is dancing in their car seat with wild abandon, and you're hacked off because their music has leaked into your space. You've made a choice to be the "get off my lawn" person rather than to share in someone else's happiness.

How we walk our daily portion of the Appalachian Trail is our choice. Look down at the mud and grime of the trail or look up to see how the sky frames the landscape. You can get happy the same way you got mad; it's your choice. Find one thing driving into work each day that exemplifies the wonderment life has to offer.

SMELLING THE ROSES
ACCELERATORS

 Briefly, describe how you go about walking the "Appalachian Trail" of life every day.

 What impact do you think your approach has on your perspective?

 List one improvement you can make in your perspective that will have positive benefits on your leadership, your work, and your life.

WALKING THE TIGHTROPE

"There's no such thing as work-life balance. There are
work-life choices, and you make them, and they have
consequences."

Jack Welch

The Bible's book of Ecclesiastes carries with it a few metric
tons of sound life advice. Two of the constant themes throughout the book are "there is nothing new under the sun" and
"practice nothing to excess." As you read through the book,
it quickly becomes apparent that humanity has the same set
of problems today as existed 3,000 years ago. One verse that
directly applies to that commonality is Ecclesiastes 10:19
(KJV): "A feast is made for laughter, and wine maketh merry,
but money answereth all things." In context, the writer of
Ecclesiastes is reminding us that, as far as earthly matters are
concerned, money is necessary for our physical needs.

That need for income extends to our families as well. The
care of my family is of utmost importance for me and is one

The Innovator's Field Guide

of my greatest responsibilities. Half of caring for our families is working to supply food, clothing, shelter, and providing advantages. It is difficult to remember that aspect of "family first" when an important meeting bars us from attending a school play or soccer game. During those times we must be satisfied with the knowledge that our hard work provides the costume for the play and the best soccer cleats on the market. But we must not use this rationale as an excuse to be an absentee parent. Make every effort to attend the dance recitals, soccer games, and cheer competitions of life. Don't be too hard on yourself when work requires that you occasionally miss.

The other lesson Ecclesiastes 10:19 gives us is that laughter and merriment are components of the good life too. Work-life balance for leaders starts by assisting our team members to achieve that in their own lives. When we assist our team with those goals, we not only find solutions for ourselves, but we also build loyalty within our team members.

Leaders from Jack Welch to Sheryl Sandberg say that work-life balance is impossible. I disagree; however, I know from experience that it's an elusive art—almost literally like walking a tightrope. To over-lean to one side, our personal lives and families suffer. To over-lean to the other, our work, our company and potentially our financial security suffer. Learn the art of tightrope walking. You'll be glad you did.

WALKING THE TIGHTROPE
ACCELERATORS

 On a scale of one to ten (one being best and ten being worst), rate yourself on the aspect of work/life balance.

 Identify two or three things you can do to make personal improvements in this regard.

 Now identify the two or three things you can do to help your team members walk the work/life tightrope more consistently and confidently.

FOCUS ON THE CORE

"As an entrepreneur, you love your business like a child, and you're taught to be laser-focused on the business."

Daymond John

In a small town, two businesses had served the same clientele for years. One of them was a grain and feed store, and the other was a hardware and tool store. Each business owner wanted to capture extra sales by dovetailing new categories of goods and providing a one-stop shopping solution for their customers. They had both heard that this tactic was being employed by chain stores and tried to emulate that formula. So, the feed store started stocking hardware items and hired an employee to oversee that category. The hardware store did the same with feed and grain items.

Both owners encountered the same problem, each from his own perspective. The feed store's clients who wanted tools were not happy with the small selection. The hardware store's owner often heard complaints from his customers about the scant inventory of grain and feed. This went on for a couple of years, and neither business owner understood why the add-on categories weren't as successful as they would have liked.

Finally, at the local meat and three, the hardware-store owner came up to the table where the feed-store man sat and said, "We need to talk." The feed-store man agreed, and by the end of lunch they worked out a solution. Each of them would not try to do something the other one did better, and each store swapped their one employee who managed the competing category. Soon, sales and customer satisfaction were up for both store owners.

Find out what you are good at, and be the best at that one thing. Diversification, if not properly executed, can be a grave distraction to yourself and your team.

FOCUS ON THE CORE

ACCELERATORS

 Take a moment to briefly describe your core business.

 Now describe the component of your core business that you are the best in the world (or in your market) at doing, which no one else can match. What other things are you trying to do that are distracting you from your core capabilities?

 What partnerships might you develop to enhance your core business, without creating unnecessary distraction?

OH YEAH, THE CUSTOMERS

"The best customer service is if the customer doesn't need
to call you, doesn't need to talk to you. It just works."

Jeff Bezos

A friend of mine owns a small business and found herself in
the enviable position of having excess liquid capital. Her business
was currently supporting her and fed her soul, but would
have been considered a flyspeck on the commercial accounts
of her bank. Currently, her excess funds were sitting in a savings
account drawing next to nothing in interest. Not being
that familiar with investments, she asked her bank's branch
manager what the bank could do to help her money grow. The
branch manager promptly replied that one of their commercial
specialists would call her to discuss her options.

A week went past and then two without a peep from the
bank's specialist. My friend closed her account with that bank
telling the branch manager the institution obviously didn't have
need of her funds. The bank had a chance to grow with her, and

they choose not to. As far as the bank was concerned, the loss of her account appeared to be insignificant. The commercial specialist, if contacted at all, triaged his or her calls to the largest accounts first and my friend obviously drew the short straw.

"Now a promise made is a debt unpaid," is a line penned by Robert Service in his poem "The Cremation of Sam McGee." (Coincidentally, Service was working at a bank when he wrote that.) When we don't deliver to a customer, we remain in their debt. Like any business, when our debt to equity ratio gets too high, there can be dire consequences.

Another similar analogy is the one of an emotional bank account. Whether we recognize it or not, when we enter into a relationship with someone, we open an emotional bank account with them. When we make more deposits than withdrawals (give to the relationship more than we take), our balance remains positive. When we make more withdrawals than deposits (take more than we give), we become "overdrawn," and experience the associated negative consequences. We all should take some time periodically to evaluate our personal customer service debt to equity ratio, or the balances of the emotional bank accounts we have with our customers, stakeholders, and teammates.

OH YEAH, THE CUSTOMERS

ACCELERATORS

 Make a list of the people who are important to your success—clients, stakeholders, teammates, etc.

 Now, place "A+" (to denote a positive bank balance), or "A-" (to denote a negative balance) next to their names.

 If you have outstanding debts or negative balances, clear them up as soon as possible.

WORDS ARE TOOLS: USE THE RIGHT ONE FOR THE RIGHT JOB

"There is a great power in words, if you don't hitch too many of them together."

Josh Billings

There is a transformative power in the language we use with our teams. If you don't believe that words are important, why do news stories waft across our feeds about a group calling for the ban of a popular book? Why do companies now have "talent management" departments instead of human resources or personnel departments? It is because the way ideas are communicated carry weight. In our businesses, the power of words sets the standard in our team's mental state. Consider a team member who comes to you with an idea you can't quite wrap your head around. There is a huge difference between saying, "I don't understand a word you've said; tell me again" and

"I'm not clear on some points; let's go over it one more time to make sure I understand." The first response's language might make your team member reluctant to come to you with ideas, whereas the second statement lets your team member know you're invested in their opinion. Furthermore, the first statement implies a problem with the idea or the manner in which it was presented. The second statement suggests the problem is with understanding of the receiver (me).

The structure of our language to team members should always hold the connotations of encouragement and growth rather than criticism and dead ends. That is the difference between saying, "What if we…" versus "That's not possible" when a clunker is thrown into the mix. The recipient is challenged when faced with a "what if" and given permission to continue their line of thought. "That's not possible" automatically tells the recipient their idea was not valid, and they will become guarded before speaking again.

If your language choices normally roll toward the dead-end spectrum, it'll take some practice to change your habits in that regard. It's been said that actions take 10,000 repetitions to form a habit (to become cataloged as "muscle memory")—the same concept is true with language choices. Develop your own personalized set of encouragement-centric language and practice its usage. This may sound contrived, but as a leader, you literally set your team's tone via your language.

WORDS ARE TOOLS: USE THE RIGHT ONE FOR THE RIGHT JOB
ACCELERATORS

 Identify the common words you use when expressing disagreement with someone or when giving constructive feedback.

 Highlight the negative terms or phrases that seem to be habitual for you.

 Identify replacement words or alternatives to these overly negative terms or phrases that are much more positive, or at the least, neutral.

METRICS MATTER!

"In business, the idea of measuring what you are doing, picking the measurements that count, like customer satisfaction and performance ... you thrive on that."

Bill Gates

In September of 1999, after traveling 416 million miles, NASA's Mars Climate Orbiter fired its thrusters, laying a course to orbit the Red Planet. Fifteen days later, the $327.6 million project burned as it hit the Martian atmosphere at an incorrect altitude and angle for a safe descent to the planet's surface. An investigation into this catastrophic crash found that despite the scores of literal rocket scientists who worked on the probe, everyone had overlooked a single mission element that caused the crash. A piece of software supplied by a subcontractor was written using English measurements, and NASA's software ran on the metric system. The software worked together perfectly, but the discrepancy in the two methods of measurement gave ground crews inaccurate data that caused the Mars Climate Orbiter to crash.

As a business leader, you must gauge performance based on measurable results. The trend of professionally living and dying by pivot-table-driven metrics has become a popular method to monitor team performance. A team's efforts to "hit the numbers" may not always align with attaining profitable goals. Are we measuring the right things, interpreting that data correctly, and communicating the results to our associates effectively and productively? Dig into those numbers with your team and find out their interpretation of the data.

Had the two Mars Climate Orbiter teams been on the same page with their measurements, the tens of thousands of man-hours that went into mission prep would have given NASA scientists years of atmospheric data to analyze. As is, the Mars Climate Orbiter landed on Martian soil as a molten heap of slag and rubble. Understanding how your set of accountability metrics affects your team could mean the difference between success and underperformance.

METRICS MATTER!

ACCELERATORS

 What drives the economic engine of your business, organization, or work group?

 What metrics do you review on a regular basis and how are they connected to these key drivers? Do you need to adjust the things you measure on a regular basis?

 In what ways could you involve your team in the collection, interpretation, and action planning about your performance metrics?

SIMPLE IS POWERFUL
AND EFFECTIVE

"No problem can be solved until it is reduced to some simple
form. The changing of a vague difficulty into a specific,
concrete form is a very essential element of thinking."

J.P. Morgan

One task that binds every business leader together is problem
solving. We are the Ann Landerses of our respective fields,
expected to be the silver bullet to slay difficulties. The sheer
number of problems we solve in a day takes a mental toll, even
if simple answers are sufficient. One method to reduce the
mental fatigue is to ask that every problem that is dropped
in your lap is explained to you as if you were a five-year-old.
Those who have been around small children for more than ten
minutes have been forced to explain complex ideas in simple
terms. We also encapsulate our explanations to the wee ones
as succinctly as possible, because the attention span of a five-
year-old is on par with that of a busy executive.

This simplification process can initially feel silly and perhaps even maddening, but a funny thing happens when you break any problem or idea down into its elemental or fundamental components. The momentous bogeyman of a problem becomes smaller and more manageable. The moving parts of the problem can then be triaged to focus on groups of smaller solutions that will form the basis of the plan.

Those that have come to you for a solution are forced to reexamine the problem in a different context as well. The act of simplifying the problem and presenting it to you in that form will often guide the team member into formulating their own solution. At that point, if no additional guidance is needed, your mental energy is spared. Your team member has been taught a skill that will eventually lead to fewer problems being laid at your feet. In that case, everyone wins!

SIMPLE IS POWERFUL
AND EFFECTIVE
ACCELERATORS

 What problems are "sitting on your desk" currently that need to be addressed?

 How can you simplify those problems down to their fundamental elements so that they can be more easily understood and solved?

 Bring your team together and engage them in the process of problem simplification and solution design.

 Create a regular forum (weekly, monthly, etc.) to bring your team together to simplify and solve the problems at hand.

DIFFERENT PERSPECTIVES, BETTER SOLUTIONS

"You have to get along with people, but you also have to recognize that the strength of a team is different people with different perspectives and different personalities."

Steve Case

Walt Disney left an indelible mark on both American culture and the entertainment industry. Out of the thousands of Disney anecdotes, one should hit home with any change agent. One of Disney's animators said of him, "There were actually three different Walts. The dreamer, the realist, and the spoiler." As leaders, we should recognize those three elements can and should exist within us all, and then manage how those different faces are presented to our teams in problem-solving exercises.

As the dreamer, we should foster the innate creativity that exists within ourselves and our teams.

The Innovator's Field Guide

As the realist, an honest evaluation of the "what if we" is translated into the either a workable plan or repurposed/retooled to fit our unique set of resources.

As the spoiler, play a different set of "what ifs" in which we identify obstacles that bar us from an optimal outcome.

Each of the three aspects of Disney must be applied consistently and evenly when approaching any problem. If we allow our teams to focus on being dreamers, without a dose of realism, the scale of our solutions could run amok. Building miniature drones to zap wasps invading the factory floor might solve a bug problem, but it's not a feasible solution. Using a small drone with a live camera feed to identify insect nests on high support columns would be a more realistic component to solving an infestation.

Mastery of the three aspects of Disney requires, like many disciplines, balance and self-examination. Only when we adjust our inner dreamer, realist, and spoiler to their proper proportions can we teach our team the same skill set. While we're collectively learning, however, we can "assign" those roles to specific team members to artificially create them on the team. Much like Edward de Bono's *Six Thinking Hats*, including our team members in this role-playing exercise is a great way to balance the three perspectives until we develop the disciplines across the team.

DIFFERENT PERSPECTIVES, BETTER SOLUTIONS
ACCELERATORS

 Which of Disney's perspectives comes most naturally to you?

 Think about how you could apply the other Disney perspectives in your team this week.

 Consider reading a copy of Edward de Bono's *Six Thinking Hats* and develop a plan to apply the principles in your next team planning session.

YOUR TRUE CALLING COMES
FROM THE INSIDE

"The first time I walked on stage, I knew that was what I was created to do. I knew that there was a calling and a sense of purpose in my life that gave me fulfillment and a sense of destiny."

T.D. Jakes

Unless you're a film buff, you may only have a nodding acquaintance with the Hedy Lamarr. The raven-haired beauty dominated the silver screen from the 1930s to the 1950s. Of the Austrian-born actress's first American film, *Algiers*, one filmgoer said when she came on screen, "everyone gasped... Lamarr's beauty literally took one's breath away." Fame and fortune based on her looks and acting talent followed Lamarr throughout her career, but she had a secret. Hedy Lamarr was a genius.

Off screen, Lamarr tinkered. She held no degree or formal training but invented a technology that improved the efficacy of traffic lights. Howard Hughes often consulted with her on aircraft designs. During World War Two, Lamarr developed a frequency-hopping signal generator for torpedoes that negated any signal-jamming efforts. This technology formed the basis for Wi-Fi and Bluetooth-capable devices today.

There are two powerful lessons we can learn from Hedy Lamarr. The first is that she never accepted that she was "just a pretty actress." The public recognized her for her films, but Hedy's experiments were known only to a few. Hedy had a sense of self and mission that negated popular perceptions. Secondly, she used her "day job" to become a vehicle to dream and explore her penchant for technology. Even if we feel like our current career or position isn't our passion, if we let those circumstances kill our soul, we can never achieve the kernel of greatness inside of us. Had Hedy Lamarr resigned herself to just being an actress, the technological landscape of today might look much different.

Everyone has a calling—a God-given purpose for why they were created. For some, their vocation is their calling. I know some pastors, counselors, health care providers, and others who make their living fulfilling their calling. For others, their vocation *supports* their calling. I suspect Hedy Lamarr was among the latter.

Believe in what is inside of you and not what others perceive you as. Connect your vocation with your calling, and you can change the world. If you struggle to believe that, think about Hedy Lamarr, "just another pretty girl" who changed our world.

OUR TRUE CALLING COMES
FROM THE INSIDE
ACCELERATORS

 What is your calling—your God-given purpose for being placed on this Earth? If you don't know, start spending the time required to discover your calling.

 How does your vocation relate to your calling? Are they synonymous? Or, does your vocation support your calling?

 In what ways can you link what you do every day to the fulfillment of your calling?

NUMBERS FIB, STATISTICS LIE!

"Facts are stubborn, but statistics are more pliable."

Mark Twain

During the darkest days of the Second World War, Allied bombers were being shot down in alarming numbers. To address those losses, a study was commissioned to examine aircraft that had returned to base damaged by enemy fire. After studying where thousands of bullets had struck aircraft, a recommendation was made to armor areas that were being hit most frequently. This would give an aircraft the maximum protection without overburdening the airframe with unnecessary armor. The logic ran sound to the upper echelons of command, but they wanted a second opinion.

One might think top bomber pilots would have been consulted, but the military turned to statistician, Abraham Wald. In this world of numerical connections and probabilities, Wald was a rock star. Wald looked at the data sets provided to him and found the highest percentage of bullet holes were in aircraft fuselages and the lowest percentage fell on engines. The military wanted confirmation from Wald that the fuselages should be armored. Wald answered with a simple question: "Where are the missing bullets?"

No one understood what Wald was getting at and asked him to explain. Wald told them that they were examining airframes that returned to base and not ones that had been shot down. Therefore, a bomber could take hits on the fuselage and return home. The engines were where armor needed to be applied. The recommendation was put into effect, and bomber losses dropped significantly.

Great innovators fall in love with the problem they're trying to solve before they fall in love with a solution. They objectively articulate their underlying assumptions and they test them relentlessly. They're willing to fire their ideas if they are deemed implausible. Wald's missing bullets illustrates that we must question our assumptions before seeking solutions and have the fortitude to speak up against flawed conventional wisdom.

26

NUMBERS FIB, STATISTICS LIE!

ACCELERATORS

- List the potential areas of flawed conventional wisdom that you have in your business, work area, or project.

- What numbers or underlying assumptions in your business do you need to re-examine?

- What are the key metrics in your business that you need to be looking at on a regular basis to ensure your business is operating effectively and efficiently?

WELCOME TO THE TANK!

"Education is what remains after one has forgotten what one has learned in school."

Albert Einstein

There is an accessible laboratory for innovation that you may never have considered taking advantage of—the reality show *Shark Tank*. The show allows small-business owners to pitch their wares to industry moguls. In return for access to their distribution chains and expertise, these tycoons usually receive equity shares in return. The show is salaciously presented, but there are underpinnings that the business-minded can learn in between the closeups and dramatic music:

N   Analyzing the sales pitches can help you refine your own persuasive arguments. Owners only have a few minutes of screen time to convey the merits of their companies and what they are seeking from the Sharks. Pick up what works well during these pitches and employ those techniques yourself.

✔ Listen to the mistakes these business owners have made in their journeys. Everything from supply chains to capitalization mistakes are vetted during pitches. You can avoid similar minefields if you pay close attention.

✔ Understand why business owners overvalue their ventures. A hefty percentage of *Shark Tank* participants either don't know the value of their business or overestimate their company's value. We all like to think that our feet don't stink, but seeing a smelly pair of gym shoes for what they are is just as important as having confidence.

✔ Evaluate the deals that are offered and the basis for which business owners accept or decline those offers. By doing so, you can fine-tune your own deal-making skills.

Once you get past the reality-TV shtick, *Shark Tank* is a learning laboratory. When you view each company as a miniature case study, the show takes on a whole new meaning. Who says TV rots your brain?

WELCOME TO THE TANK!

ACCELERATORS

 Identify two or three TV Shows, YouTube Channels, podcasts, or other media most closely related to your product, innovation, or business. What new things can you learn from them?

 Carve out time and make it a priority to consume these media regularly.

 Keep a notepad close at hand to analyze and record the lessons learned from each episode.

GO AHEAD,
BREAK A RULE!

"You are remembered for the rules you break."

Douglas MacArthur

A few years back, Robert Fulghum's book *All I Really Need to Know I Learned in Kindergarten* was all the rage. Fulghum's text does remind us that simple actions like cleaning up our messes and playing fair are the keys to a good life. While Fulghum is certainly correct in his assertion that applying childhood lessons to adult situations is applicable, there is a danger in this philosophy. In kindergarten, we were conditioned to think that, above all else, we should follow the rules. As leaders, one of our unspoken mandates is to know when to break the rules.

If that statement conjured Scooby Doo howling "Huuuhhh?" in your mind, think about how well following established procedures worked for the folks at United Airlines in the spring of 2017. The forceable removal of a passenger randomly chosen on a full flight to free up seats for a United aircrew did irreparable damage to the company's image. All the United associates involved in resolving that situation followed company procedures to the letter. If someone had had the courage to break the rules and diffuse the situation, things might have turned out differently for the United brand.

Manuals, procedures, and common practices are not sacred tomes designed to cover the nuances of every situation. As leaders, we must be willing to do what's right when our guidelines fall short. Yes, there can be professional consequences for going rogue. However, the rewards of judicious rule breaking can benefit you and your organization. I can guarantee that the Board of United now wishes someone had broken the rules that day in 2017.

GO AHEAD,
BREAK A RULE!
ACCELERATORS

 What rules in your business, organization, or industry need to be challenged?

 How can you go about challenging those rules in a manner that limits downside risks, but creates the greatest upside potential?

 Prioritize three major rules that need to be challenged and take the appropriate steps to challenge them. Once you're done, move on to the next three.

WHEN COMFORT KILLS

"A higher rate of urgency does not imply ever-present panic, anxiety, or fear. It means a state in which complacency is virtually absent."

John Kotter

Military analogies, anecdotes, and terminology prodigiously worm their way into business texts. Rarely do these loosely based parallels address the greatest lesson to be learned from armed conflict—vision. Historical examples abound of generals fighting the last battle in a current conflict. None better exemplify this than the World War One's British General Douglas Haig's statement:

> I believe that the value of the horse and the opportunity for the horse in the future are likely to be as great as ever. Aeroplanes and tanks are only accessories to the men and the horse.

Commissioned as a cavalry officer, Haig served in the Sudan and Boer War, where cavalry units often turned the tide of a skirmish. Haig's comfort zone was with cavalry, and there he stayed. During the 1916 Somme Offensive, Haig called for a full-frontal assault. His plan was to have infantry punch a hole in German lines and then send cavalry through the middle to envelop the enemy's flanks. The four-month offensive cost the British 420,000 lives and Haig's forces captured only six miles of German-held ground.

Holding on to outmoded techniques and failing to envision any tool's potential is a trap we, like Haig, can easily fall into. The coziness of the familiar is a lullaby that sucks us into the belief that relevance can be co-opted easily by old methods. If you're satisfied with what was, there's no need to look for inspiration. You're already where you want to be. If you're not at that place, ask yourself with every change how General Haig would view that innovation and do the exact opposite.

WHEN COMFORT KILLS

ACCELERATORS

 Give deep consideration for a moment or two about the degree of complacency that exists in your life and work right now.

 In what areas of your work, business, or organization is complacency obvious?

 Identify three specific areas where complacency is a problem and develop a plan to shake things up a bit.

DON'T DRINK THE POISON!

"The best revenge is massive success."

Frank Sinatra

CNBC's co-host of *The Deed*, Sean Conlon, has a "typical" rags-to-riches story. The Irish immigrant worked a five-dollar-an-hour janitorial job while breaking into the highly competitive Chicago real-estate market. Working one-hundred-hour weeks, developing a nasty ulcer because of his dogged attention to detail, and coming up with a new formula for developing and selling commercial real estate netted Conlon $55 million in sales four years after putting down his broom. But that's not what is "atypical" about Sean Conlon.

The real-estate business is acutely cutthroat and getting the shaft on commissions is not uncommon. According to Conlon he's been on the ethical underside of deals thousands of times. One particular time he showed a "for sale by owner" house to a client just because he thought the house might fit the client's needs. Come to find out the house was owned by a real-estate broker. The client bought the house, and Conlon gets stiffed on the commission. Conlon let the slight go and adopted the philosophy of:

> Don't put all of your energy into trying to get them back. Keep winning. Get up and go back at it every day.

Professional malice does you no favors. The effort you spend seething only hurts you. In fact, it's been said that failing to forgive is like drinking poison and expecting the other person to die.

As for Conlon, six years later his company worked a deal with the broker who had not cut him a commission check years earlier. Conlon was looking over the deal's paperwork, recognized the broker's name, and shaved his commission accordingly for the six-year-old slight. Your own personal success is the best revenge you can ever exact.

DON'T DRINK THE POISON!
ACCELERATORS

 Against whom do you hold a grudge or hard feelings that have proven difficult for you to overcome? What were the offenses that caused the grudge(s)?

 What success(es) would be the greatest, most constructive "revenge" you could have in those situations?

 Develop and implement a plan to make those successes a reality. Once you start working on the plan, make a decision to forgive and forget those past offenses.

TEAM SUCCESSES ARE
LEADER SUCCESSES

"The secret to success is good leadership, and good leadership is all about making the lives of your team members or workers better."

Tony Dungy

I once heard of a business leader who was fond of saying he was constantly trying to work himself out of a job. When pressed on the meaning of the enigmatic phrase, he said it related to his perceptions of team development. The better his team was at performing their job duties, the less they needed him for guidance in day-to-day matters. When he had developed a team that no longer required his leadership, he had effectively "worked himself out of his job." Any of his team members could seamlessly step into his job role, and both he and the team members could advance to the next challenge.

This point may never come with some teams, but what a grand example of servant leadership. Working your way out of a job is not the path of least resistance for a leader. It's infinitely easier to ding team members on their missteps and show your superiors how you've held the team accountable. While accountability is a necessary component of any team, accountability for the sake of covering one's lack of team development is a copout.

To be a true leader, one must check his ego at the door and embrace the notion that team successes are personal leadership successes as well. One must not be threatened by a team member's individual achievements. Rather, true leaders recognize their measure of success is based on how well their team performs. That requires "working yourself out of a job," and in doing so, you will be working yourself into your next job.

TEAM SUCCESSES ARE
LEADER SUCCESSES
ACCELERATORS

 In what areas can your team excel if you were to develop them and let them go?

 How can you make the lives of your team members better?

 Make a plan to improve the lives of your team members, to develop them to their fullest potential, and then step back and let it happen.

AUTHENTICITY MATTERS

"Heroes are never perfect, but they're brave, they're authentic, they're courageous, determined, discreet, and they've got grit."

Wade Davis

Quantum physics is freakishly difficult to understand. The particles that make up an atom don't behave based on the set of Newton's Laws we all learned in high school. Simply observing a subatomic particle can change its behavior. There's a famous quantum-mechanics trial known as the double-slit experiment. Electrons are shot at a barrier containing two slits. One would expect that on the other side of the barrier, the electrons would form a single type of pattern. In the world of quantum mechanics, there can be two distinct patterns formed by the electrons depending on if the experiment is observed or not observed. As hocus pocus as it sounds, on a quantum level matter changes behavior based solely on observation or the lack thereof.

People act in much the same way as electrons. Our behavior patterns are different when we know someone has their eye on us. When guests are coming over, we clean an already spotless house. When the boss is around, we modify our behavior to become what we think our superior wants, or we shellac whatever they're checking on. Everyone wants to put their best foot forward. When we put on a face for others that differs from our day-to-day self, a problem arises. As a leader, our team members see this well-intentioned, but ultimately duplicitous behavior and feel that it is appropriate to mimic it—with others and with you.

Be yourself, warts and all. You've heard it all your life, but that doesn't give you permission to not work on your warts. The more authentic you are with yourself and others, the more genuine they will be with you. As a side note… keep an eye on quantum-mechanics-related technology. Like the prediction of plastics in *The Graduate*, it is the future.

AUTHENTICITY MATTERS
ACCELERATORS

 In what areas of your life, business, or organization to you tend to whitewash reality?

 What would be the consequences of being authentic in those areas? What are you afraid of?

 How can you make the necessary changes in those areas so that you can be authentic, without fear?

COLLABORATION ONLY MAKES THINGS BETTER

"When you need to innovate, you need collaboration."

Marissa Mayer

Westmoreland, Tennessee, is not where one would expect to find success. On average the unemployment rate of this Middle Tennessee town has trended above the national rate since 1990. Decades of mistrust between the Westmoreland haves and have-nots fostered division and a profound lack of cooperation. These splits created 30 churches and non-profit organizations in an area where less than 10,000 people lived. Each group had its own food pantry to try to meet the needs of the low-income residents of the area, and still many in Westmoreland went hungry.

All of that started to change ten years ago, when a collaborative effort was set up almost accidentally by an outsider. Minister Charlie Millson worked to find common ground among the disparate groups. Millson appealed to the one thing these different groups had in common—they all lacked funding. Within one week of moving to the area, Millson devised a plan and explained it by saying:

> We knew that the small churches didn't have the funding, manpower, or sometimes even the space to stock a pantry. Many of the churches didn't even have telephones where those in need could reach the pantries.

Millson called a meeting of some of the town leaders and proposed that they pool their resources into a new organization, the Westmoreland Food Bank. He found an inexpensive place to rent in the downtown area and opened a food bank with regular hours and trained volunteers. Soon churches started sending volunteers and resources. Now almost every church in the area participates in the food bank, and it serves over 600 families each month. All of this was financed and staffed by locals in a town where collaboration was unknown until someone helped the people see the benefits of working together.

COLLABORATION ONLY MAKES THINGS BETTER
ACCELERATORS

 Identify the areas in your business or organization where there is uncoordinated activity (at best) to vast disagreement (at worst).

 Prioritize those areas from the most critical to the least critical according to their impact on your collective success.

 Develop a plan to address the most critical by pulling everyone together and building a plan that requires collaboration—one that everyone buys into.

WHAT ARE THEY SAYING ABOUT YOU?

"It is surprising how little most small business values the customers. A positive feedback from the customer is critical to your business, and what's more important is their referral."

Fabrizio Moreira

A major grocery store chain performed a series of focus-group studies to ascertain what constituted a good shopping experience. Everyone in the organization expected the results would include items like short checkout lines, an attentive staff, and an outstanding product selection at a reasonable price. When the study data was tallied, predictably all those items were high on the customers' mental checklists. There was one item that did take the executive group by surprise—bathroom cleanliness. Customers overwhelmingly believed that if a grocery store's bathroom was dirty, the staff was not paying much attention to the fresh food items the store sold. Many in the executive group had rarely been in a store's bathroom because they were focused on sales floor operations and presentation.

New equipment was purchased, and specialized training was put into place to ensure this chain's bathrooms were always pristine. After implementation, customers still perceived the chain's bathrooms were not clean. Why? The executives had money in their budgets for the capital expenditures but were unwilling to increase stores' labor budgets. The already thinly staffed stores had scads of new cleaning equipment, but no labor hours to use it.

Listening to customers' feedback doesn't mean wedging in their expectations with our metrics. To grow, the metrics must align with the needs of our customers. In the case of this grocery chain, they did add hours into store operations for bathroom cleaning. At the end of the day, the executives found that in stores with higher cleanliness ratings, the customers spent more time in their stores. As customer "in-store" time increased, so did profits.

WHAT ARE THEY SAYING
ABOUT YOU?
ACCELERATORS

 What would your customers say about you if you were to ask them some open-ended questions about their impressions of your business?

 How might you put a process together to gather and act on regular feedback from your customers? (Research "Talking to Humans.") Develop and implement a plan to get initial feedback from your clients over a period of time and then refine it into an ongoing process.

BUILT TO LAST

"The greatest legacy one can pass on to one's children and grandchildren is not money or other material things accumulated in one's life, but rather a legacy of character and faith."

Billy Graham

Robert Bigelow will be the first to admit that the nearly $300 million of his own money he's sunk into Bigelow Aerospace is the worst financial decision he's ever made. He knew that going into the venture. The founder of Budget Suites of America made his fortune on low-budget, long-term stay rental apartments, and some would say, is now frittering his money away on a pipe dream. With no background in science, Bigelow bought a research project from NASA and has literally expanded on the idea.

Bigelow Aerospace produces inflatable habitats that can be used in orbit and potentially on other planets. NASA had tinkered with the idea for years and scrapped the project in 2000. Bigelow saw the potential and snapped up patents for the inflatable habitats for dimes on the dollar. In 2016, a Bigelow habitat was attached to the International Space Station as a proof of concept and it works as advertised: a cheap, self-sustaining (well, as self-sustaining as anything can be in space), and lightweight habitat that could pave the way for humanity's first steps in colonizing our solar system.

He's constantly catcalled by the press for both his highly public stance on his company's product and for his belief that UFOs have visited Earth. Robert Bigelow doesn't care a whit about what others think of him. He's thinking in terms of a legacy that will allow mankind the kind of inspiration we haven't seen since the first moon landing in 1969. That's some vision from a man who got his start in cheap hotels.

The lessons from Bigelow are numerous, but building something that lasts longer than he will is the key point. We can't take it with us. Have you ever seen a hearse pulling a U-Haul? We can, however, make sure we're paving the way for those who will come after us.

BUILT TO LAST
ACCELERATORS

 What's your legacy? On what part of the world will you leave your unique thumbprint?

 How does your business, product, or innovation contribute to the fulfillment of your personal legacy? Is it your legacy? Does it support your legacy?

 Spend the time necessary to draw and internalize (deeply understand) the clear link between your business, product, or innovation and the legacy you wish to leave behind.

ACTION IN THE FACE OF FEAR

"I learned that courage was not the absence of fear, but the triumph over it. The brave man is not he who does not feel afraid, but he who conquers that fear."

Nelson Mandela

Are you old enough to remember when your local news station touted its weather forecaster because you wanted to know if your weekend plans were going to get rained out? Pay attention the next time the tagline for the meteorologist hits your screen. One of my local network affiliate touts:

> Your top source for *severe* [emphasis mine] weather coverage and the most reliable local forecast information.

The buzzwords "severe weather" coming before "reliable" is no mistake. You've been hooked into watching because of the fear of life-threatening weather and your wish to avoid it. It's not just the local weather—the news is rife with taglines that appeal to fear avoidance. In short, fear sells.

It's no wonder that faced with media designed to induce the basest of instincts, fear is the number-one reason most people also never achieve their goals or aspirations. They're afraid of sticking their neck out. They're afraid of falling flat. They're afraid of looking foolish. If that's you, STOP IT. In the words of the great Zig Ziglar:

> F–E–A–R has two meanings: 'Forget Everything and Run' or 'Face Everything and Rise.' The choice is yours.

It's been estimated that 85% of that about which we worry never happens. Of the remaining 15%, the vast majority of people say when that fear does come to fruition, it brings with it benefits or personal lessons that were more valuable than harmful. That means only about 3% of the time that which we fear comes to pass and could be potentially harmful. A full 97% of the time, we're fearful of something that has a low probability of causing harm.

If fear is a barrier for you, start building confidence blocks that have nothing to do with your business. Go whitewater rafting, bungee jumping, or skydiving. Anything that you've always wanted to do, but are afraid to do—get to it. The activity doesn't have to be grandiose, but those confidence blocks will build upon each other to wall away other fears that are keeping you from your dreams.

ACTION IN THE FACE OF FEAR
ACCELERATORS

 Write down your three biggest fears either inside, or outside your business or organization.

 Identify opportunities to face those fears head-on.

 Develop a plan to take advantage of those opportunities and prove to yourself once and for all that our fears are often bigger and meaner than reality.

ACCIDENTAL SUCCESS

"Many of life's failures are people who did not realize how close they were to success when they gave up."

Thomas A. Edison

I'd like to present a unique investment opportunity in Unadulterated Food Products. They're an upstart juice company based in Brooklyn, but as part of full disclosure, the chairman didn't finish high school. He also has no background in the food and beverage industry. He and his partners know as much about the beverage business as they do about building an atom bomb. The chairman, since his teens he… well… washed windows and graduated to a window-washing brokerage company. But, boy, he's got moxie and their flagship product is a one hundred percent naturally carbonated apple juice. They accidentally let one of the batches ferment last week, and it popped the tops on all the bottles, but you've got to break a few eggs to make an omelet, don't you? How much would you like to invest? Oh… you're not interested. I understand.

Imagine that pitch was given to you in 1972 and you had the foreknowledge that Unadulterated Food Products would turn into Snapple. That dropout window washer was Hyman Golden, who would make a cool $100 million when Snapple was sold to Quaker in 1994. Golden and his partner's vision was to produce beverages that were made from all-natural ingredients for health-food stores. The brand branched out into iced teas and became a cultural phenomenon in the late 1980s and early 1990s. Quaker's subsequent failings in producing and marketing the Snapple brand had nothing to do with Golden or his partners.

Golden and his partners built a company using "the best stuff on Earth" and were bought out for $1.7 billion. Never underestimate someone with vision and a dream. *Now* can I interest you in investing in Unadulterated Food Products?

ACCIDENTAL SUCCESS
ACCELERATORS

 List three to five failures or setbacks you've had with your product, innovation, or business in the past couple of years.

 Take some time to analyze and write down the root cause(s) of each failure or setback.

 Now prioritize those prior setbacks or failures as to which ones are worth trying again.

 Develop a plan for each, making certain you address the root cause of the previous failure as you chart your course to success.

HELP YOURSELF TO SOME "ME" TIME

"If you are feeling some December blues, or even depression, don't fight it. Instead, do something for yourself. Be reflective. Let the emotions exist. And be encouraged that, like me, you can get to a better place, but it can take time."

Brad Feld

I once heard it said that everyone has a finite amount of love they can spend each day. Of course, we're not talking about romantic love, but the love that is the underlying the care we project onto the people and events surrounding us. We all have a limited capacity of what we can pour of ourselves into anything. Careers, families, hobbies, and simply being an adult make withdrawals from our daily love allotment. If you think that's not the case, remember the last time you thought, "If my phone rings one more time today, I'll scream." When you've hit the point of elevated frustration, you've spent all the love you can. Outward signs of anger, eye-rolls, heavy sighs, and poor decisions are then sure to follow.

There is a slight fallacy in the "finite amount of love to spend each day" theorem. The maxim is true if we don't consider that our output of love can be revitalized in a day by taking time for ourselves. You are your most important resource. On first brush, that statement might sound egotistical and self-centered, but it's founded on the thought that, if you don't take care of yourself, you cannot take care of anyone else. This is the same rationale behind airline emergency briefings advising you to, in the event of depressurization, put your own mask on before helping others. It's why paramedics are almost brainwashed to ensure the "scene is safe" before they go charging in to save everyone.

When driven to distraction, take fifteen minutes to do something that is all about you. Turn off your cell phone and then take a walk; knock off two hours early and go fishing, hit golf balls, or whatever it is that makes you feel like you again. Try that once and see how you feel when you come back. You'll likely have a different perspective on your day.

HELP YOURSELF TO
SOME "ME" TIME
ACCELERATORS

N What evidence do you leave behind that suggests you are just about at your wit's end?

N What activities make you feel recharged?

N How can you build those activities into your regular weekly routine?

N What triggers can you place around you to remind you of this need?

THE LEADER IN THE CORNER OFFICE

"He who stands aloof runs the risk of believing himself better than others and misusing his critique of society as an ideology for his private interests."

Theodor Adorno

There's a reason why the CBS reality series *Undercover Boss* has been on the air for eight seasons. The show places a chain-store executive or owner of a large company in an entry-level position within their own company. The series' first episode reached 38.6 million viewers, and the *New York Daily News* review tagged *Undercover Boss* as "an hour of feel-good television for underappreciated workers."

Part of the show's success is undoubtedly the *schadenfreude* of bosses slogging it out in the corporate trenches. The takeaway for leaders and the main component of the show's longevity is the underlying need for associates to feel like their efforts matter and are understood by the "folks upstairs."

If the majority of America's business leaders were successfully executing the concepts of team development and servant leadership, *Undercover Boss* wouldn't have lasted through its first season.

I'm not suggesting you should be able to perform every task of your team—you build a team to allow you to grow the company. Consider what your team members would do if you offered to work a day performing their job duties. Would your team members not give the offer a second thought because you're already ingrained in their work processes? Would they believe that you were out of touch enough not to know how or what they do? If the answer is the latter, a reevaluation of your role could be in order. Taking the time to understand the "nuts and bolts" of your company's work processes will not only build loyalty to you as a leader, but your perspective could lead to new efficiencies your team members had never considered. NBA Hall of Famer Larry Bird once said that "Leadership is diving for a loose ball, getting the crowd involved, getting other players involved. It's being able to take it as well as dish it out. That's the only way you're going to get respect from the other players."

In a nutshell, leadership requires rolling up your sleeves and getting your hands dirty. It means that you're willing to dive in after a loose ball.

THE LEADER IN THE
CORNER OFFICE
ACCELERATORS

 How close are you to the action of your team?

 What would your team say about your understanding of their roles, responsibilities, processes, and outputs?

 Where should you engage with your team to learn a little more about what they do?

MAKING QUALITY PERSONAL

"Almost all quality improvement comes via simplification of design, manufacturing ... layout, processes, and procedures."

Tom Peters

Does the phrase "process quality" make your head spin? Do acronyms like ISO, TQM, PDCA, BPR, and OQM and the associated flowcharts and hours in hotel banquet halls watching PowerPoints make you wonder if you will ever implement the new gold standard for evaluation? Put away the checklists and certification manuals for a moment. Let's start off with a new acronym for any process quality procedure, KISS (Keep it simple, stupid).

Your natural inclination for certification or recertification in any of these methodologies is to run back to your team, shouting, "Here's what we've got to do by X date!" Passing out checklists like they're Halloween candy will only serve to overload your team. As the kids today say, "You need to slow your roll." The first question your team members will ask is,

"How am I supposed to get this done with X, Y, and Z on my plate?" Be ready to answer this question by distilling the necessary actions for each of your team members (as well as the rationale) and be proactive by providing an individual plan for each team member's success.

Make this plan as simple as possible for your team members. Assign compliance tasks that are tangential to the work team members are already performing. Use the buddy system where possible to complement team members' strengths and weaknesses. Above all else, your individual plans should convey the tangible benefits each team member will receive by implementing the process quality procedures—improved efficiencies, increased customer satisfaction, or any other trigger that will get a team member excited about the process. No one likes to view another checklist as busy work so the folks upstairs can tout a certification.

The more you simplify the methodology and explain the rewards to your team, the easier any implementation or recertification will be. If you're a startup and you're thinking this particular accelerator doesn't apply to you, know that quality, repeatable processes are critical to any scalable business or innovation. Ignore them at your peril …

MAKING QUALITY PERSONAL

ACCELERATORS

 Take some time to identify the top five business processes in your business or organization that need to be improved, standardized, and documented.

 Now identify the various resources available from which you can learn the best way to improve, standardize, and document those critical processes.

 Bring your team into the learning and planning process. Get them on board, tell them why, solicit their input, and work together to make these top five processes the best in the business. Once you're done, move on to the next five, and the next five, and so on.

MEETING IN STYLE

"People who enjoy meetings should not be in charge of anything."

Thomas Sowell

Meetings are an essential component of quality communications in any business. The impact of face-to-face communications can be drastically reduced if the tool isn't used judiciously. No one wants to attend a meeting that could have been handled through another method of communication, or have a topic addressed in an email that required the dynamics of a group discussion. Here are some tips for increasing both the productivity and efficacy of face time:

🗲 Rumor has it that British Prime Minister Margret Thatcher held status update meetings where everyone stood. Her theory was that when reporting to her each participant would refrain from pontificating needlessly if they were not sitting in comfy chairs.

✎ Immediately kill any discussions in interdepartmental meetings that do not apply to the entire group.

✎ Send a meeting agenda (even an informal one) the day before the meeting is scheduled to occur. This allows team members the chance to address specific concerns before the meeting, and it keeps a tight rein on the time management of the meeting.

✎ Limit meeting topics to areas that require personal emphasis or teach a new skill/procedure, or where a group discussion would create synergistic thought.

✎ Unless personal electronic devices are salient to the meeting, have a "power down" policy.

✎ Never have deli trays or sweet goods available during the meeting. It's a nice thought, but constant grazing along the treat line is disruptive and prolongs pertinent progress.

✎ Carefully consider the attendees. Did you invite only those who would benefit from the presented topics?

✒ Send out a follow-up email detailing points that were discussed and resolutions made no more than a day after the meeting.

As for a tactic to quell the person that always asks irrelevant questions… that's your call. Just keep in mind that every minute your team is away at a meeting, their productivity goes down. Design your meetings to get the maximum ROI on their investment of time.

MEETING IN STYLE
ACCELERATORS

 On a scale of one to ten, how effective would you say your meeting management is?

 What are the top three problems with most of your meetings or meeting management?

 What steps can you take now to increase the effectiveness of your meetings?

MAKING THE ROUNDS

"My style will be management by being on the street, management by walking around. Third persons won't have to tell me what's going on in our city. I'll hear it, I'll see it, I'll touch it myself."

Carl Stokes

Denise managed fifty people in three different departments. Every morning she arrived at the office ahead of her team, grabbed a cup of coffee, and started her day. Tucked away in her cubicle, she wrapped up the unfinished business from the day before and set the agenda for the current day's business. Everyone knew Denise was in the office because the icon on the in-house instant messenger was green. She would always take the time to listen to her team members when they came to her with an issue. Denise was a competent, hardworking, and knowledgeable manager who was constantly blindsided by issues cropping up in her departments.

In Denise's case, her team tried not to bother her. Her team perceived that Denise was always too busy to come to her with small problems. Had Denise heard about the small problems, larger issues could have been avoided. She shared the same 3200-square-foot section of the office her team did and had no problems with communicating—via messenger and email throughout the day. However, Denise's team rarely had personal contact with their leader. What Denise failed to recognize is six words can be more impactful to you and your team than anything else you will do or say all day.

"Good morning; how are things going?"

The simple act of walking around your areas of responsibility and greeting your team sets the tone for the day. Your team members will tell you things that they are reluctant to email or message. In some cases, the trepidation comes from having an official record of a minor issue. Moreover, a leader's physical presence and greeting strengthens your bonds and will put your team at ease to speak more freely. The more open your team is, the more rapidly you will find out about problems and successes. Isn't that worth a few minutes to make the rounds and say, "Good morning"?

MAKING THE ROUNDS
ACCELERATORS

 How often do you walk around and authentically connect with your teammates?

 If you have a remote team, in what ways can you connect with them on a regular basis?

 What automated reminders and memory joggers can you put in place to remind you to get out of your office to "walk among the troops"?

RESULTS AND RELATIONSHIPS

"Our minds influence the key activity of the brain, which then influences everything; perception, cognition, thoughts and feelings, personal relationships; they're all a projection of you."

Deepak Chopra

Herman was the type of guy who could negotiate multimillion-dollar deals with a bulldog-like determination and a razor-sharp focus. He had that drive, that charisma, that "Midas touch" about him that drew people into his orbit, temporarily. Herman even had a beautiful wife and four wonderful children. The corporate salesman would have no need for this book because he needed no advice nor external motivation. He was a "legend in his own mind."

Herman had it all, including a disease that would eventually kill him and an anger issue to match his illness step by step. Even before his diagnosis, Herman made everyone else in his life miserable. His kids avoided him, and his wife wanted little to do with him. There were times when his family wanted to wring his neck because he brought the same determination and doggedness that served him so well in business to his personal relationships.

When Herman realized that his pursuit of business pushed away everything truly important, it was too late. His children grew up and wanted no relationship with him. His wife concluded that she would always be in second place in his heart behind his business, and she moved on. Those who drove past Herman's palatially empty house would sometimes see him sitting on the porch by himself. A month before he succumbed to the disease, Herman still posted the top sales figures at his firm. Even with that accomplishment, few people mourned his passing. Those in his office didn't miss their compatriot; they were just glad his accounts were freed up.

Successful people understand the necessary balance between Results and Relationships. If we focus on one, at the expense of the other, we lose them both. What good is it for someone to gain the whole world, yet forfeit his/her soul? If you could ask Herman you might find out.

43

RESULTS AND RELATIONSHIPS

ACCELERATORS

- Are you a Results person or a Relationships person?

- If you're a Results person, identify the specific ways in which you tend to alienate the necessary Relationships in your life.

- If you are a Relationships person, identify ways that you can develop a strong focus on delivering the necessary Results in your life.

- Make a plan to develop (and maintain) a better balance between Results and Relationships.

TO DECIDE OR NOT TO DECIDE?

"The way to develop decisiveness is to start right where you are, with the very next question you face."

Napoleon Hill

There's a little red blinking light that goes off in the corner of our eye when we are asked to decide. The longer we pause in coming up with a solution or making a decision, that blinking light flashes faster and faster. They're waiting… They need to know… now!

Here's a news flash: every decision does not have to be made on the spot. Just like saying "no," there is a power in taking the time to decide when an answer is not immediately necessary. Many "off-the-cuff" decisions can be terrible ideas that spawn from the perceived pressure exerted on you by the person seeking an answer. Should you delay making a decision, set a timetable that your response will be given and stick to it.

What you have actually done by delaying a decision is practiced time management. You have delineated how critical the problem is by setting your own timetable. You have the luxury of contemplating, researching, or asking advice in setting your decision timetable. All of this, of course, is based on your accurately triaging the problem at hand. Deciding if you should purchase printer toner from another supplier is vastly different from being faced with a Hindenburg-sized disaster.

If you are delaying because you have trouble making decisions, that's another issue. In those instances, delaying can be a crutch. If you have a pattern of latent decisiveness, it must be addressed. You cannot always rely on the luxury of time. However, taking time to reflect and research options is not necessarily being indecisive. You are indecisive if you do not follow up with that decision or waffle on a decision you've already made. Henry Kissinger once said, "Competing pressures tempt one to believe that an issue deferred is a problem avoided; more often, it is a crisis invited." Poignant words for those who often delay their decisions.

TO DECIDE OR NOT TO DECIDE?

ACCELERATORS

 Briefly describe your pattern of decision-making. Are you normally decisive? Indecisive?

 Reflect on a decision you made too quickly—one that ended up being the wrong decision.

 Now reflect on a decision you delayed—one that ended up being a crisis because of your indecisiveness.

 Now reflect on an impending decision. Take the steps to ensure this one is the right one!

PLANNING FOR THE INEVITABLE

> "I spent thirty years getting ready for that decision that took thirty seconds."
>
> General James "Chaos" Mattis

Wisdom can be found in the most unlikely of places. In the Amazon original series, *The Man in the High Castle*, a Japanese trade minister mystically remarks, "Fate is fluid. Destiny is in the hands of men." In a Western mindset, we often think the words "fate" and "destiny" are interchangeable. This is not the case. In this context, destiny is the accrual of one's efforts toward a specific goal. Few people see the years of preparation that go into becoming an overnight success. Fate is the collection of seemingly random occurrences that happen within one's day. Bumping into someone who spills their coffee on you fifteen minutes before an important meeting is fate. In this situation, the person who focuses on destiny would have a change of clothes in their car—just in case.

The contrast between fate and destiny can be reframed as reactive versus proactive thinking. A reactive thinker manages the omnipresent chaos that plagues the everyday. A proactive thinker plays the "what if" game to develop contingency strategies to overcome that chaos to achieve success. One might think this is preparing for failure. It is not. The facts are clear—successful people have a future orientation. A defensive driver imagines the future actions of other drivers based on observed behaviors and adjusts his or her driving accordingly. Foreseeing potential dangers doesn't mean a defensive driver is planning to run off the road, but they are taking steps to ensure they arrive at their destination safely.

Planning for every little potential disaster isn't possible either and is an exercise in paranoia and futility. With any project, identify the top five worst-case scenarios and develop a rough idea of how to overcome those obstacles or setbacks. Especially pay attention when you hear team members say, "Well, that will never happen." Chances are "it" will happen but you'll be ready to seize your destiny instead of being a victim of fate.

PLANNING FOR THE INEVITABLE
ACCELERATORS

 What are the major risks facing your current project, innovation, or business?

 What is the likelihood of those risks coming to fruition?

 What steps can you take to prevent those risks from happening, or to respond effectively to them when they do?

The Innovator's Field Guide

DISRUPTING THE UNIVERSE

"The reasonable man adapts himself to the world; the unreasonable one persists in trying to adapt the world to himself. Therefore, all progress depends on the unreasonable man."

George Bernard Shaw

"Do I dare disturb the universe?" were words penned by world-class poet T. S. Eliot in "The Love Song of J. Alfred Prufrock." The poem centers around the titular character observing life events happening around him and then stolidly talking himself out of participating. Prufrock makes the excuses that he's too old, too bald, or plainly too scared to pursue the things in life that interest him, comforting himself with promises that there will be time for all those things—later. Sound familiar?

Just as a J. Alfred Prufrock exists within all of us, so does our ability to disturb or disrupt the universe. As innovators, entrepreneurs, and change agents, we tend to think in terms of "disrupting" instead of "disturbing." Regardless, we often think that upsetting cosmic balances takes a cataclysmic event, but the universe can be disrupted with a phone call, email, or simply speaking up in a meeting. When our sights are only set on monumental tasks, are we using this as a cover or an excuse? Have you ever said, "When I finish Project X, everything will fall into place," as a fear-filled mask for effecting small changes?

Do one thing a day that disrupts your universe. If you do one thing a day that combats the muttering internal negative voices that hold you back, soon you'll have a catalog of universe disruptions to staunch the harshest of inner critics. Do you dare disrupt the universe? You bet you do, because the universe isn't about to change on its own. That change starts with a choice. You can choose the status quo, or you can choose to shake things up. That all begins with asking yourself every day, "How will I disrupt the universe today?"

DISRUPTING THE UNIVERSE
ACCELERATORS

 What needs disrupting in the universe around you?

 What actions can you *take right now* that will be disruptive to the universe?

 How can you create the habit of disrupting the universe each day?

SERVANT LEADERSHIP

"I believe in servant leadership, and the servant always asks, 'Where am I needed most?'"

Mike Pence

Faith is as much a key to business success as capitalization. We have faith in our vendors to supply goods on time. We have faith in our abilities and our vision. We have faith God is showing us the correct path for our lives. But do the team members we shepherd understand that we have faith in them as well? Perhaps you just bristled at my question and thought, "Of course, my team knows I trust them. They wouldn't be on my team if I didn't!"

Your associates transfer their own hopes and fears onto what you may perceive as the most insignificant of actions or words. As harsh as it sounds, there are members of your team who do not have the drive to rise to the next level on their own, as a result of their personal insecurities. Associates who fall into this category are extremely susceptible to what you may consider an insignificant slight. You may correct a team member's minor mistake in front of another team member. To you, the correction was a reflexive response to keep a small gaffe from growing into a larger problem. For the insecure team member, this sends the message that you have no faith in their abilities.

If you try to follow the principles of servant leadership, yet see this situation as babysitting or handholding, perhaps a self-examination is in order. Your job is to empower, enable, and lift those in your care. Some members of your team need extra attention in areas that are not defined on quarterly evaluations. Open your eyes to the personal issues your team members have and adjust your actions accordingly. This may just be where you are needed most today.

SERVANT LEADERSHIP

ACCELERATORS

 Reflect on your recent or routine interactions with your associates. Are there any situations that come to mind where you may have left the wrong impression about your faith and trust in them?

 Thinking more about those interactions, identify one or two associates whom you know to experience the insecurities described above.

 Put a plan in place to not only demonstrate that you believe in them, but also to help them overcome these insecurities. Start taking consistent action now.

WHEN YOUR PASSION GETS
YOU IN TROUBLE

"There is no passion to be found in playing small—in settling
for a life that is less than the one you are capable of living."

Nelson Mandela

I've taught my daughters for years to "find something you love
to do and then figure out how to get paid for it, and you'll
never have to work a day in your life." Gavin believed in that
adage as well.

He was the rare combination of right and left brain and
double-majored in art and finance. While Gavin was content sussing out future values and P/E ratios, his passion lay
within art. Doodling, sculpting, painting, it mattered not what
medium he worked with. If his creative side was channeled,
Gavin was happy.

Fresh from receiving his degrees, Gavin opened an
art-supply store in his metropolitan hometown. He had the

background, financing, and location to make the store successful. The prospects of competing against the chain stores and online merchants didn't faze Gavin much. He was charismatic and shared his love of art with his customers. The store held classes and art exhibits for customers of any skill level. The art-supply store became a community unto itself. Yet, within five years, the store was padlocked, and Gavin was broke.

What happened? The same presence of traditional and online competition existed as it had the day the store's doors opened. The niche market for the store's business model had not gone away; in fact, the city Gavin called home was experiencing a booming economy and influx of new residents. Market forces weren't at work in the store's demise. In fact, local market realities suggested the story should have been in growth mode.

The answer lies within his passion for his work. Gavin became his own customer. He forgot that he was running a business, and became one of his best clients. He spent so much time, and company money, enjoying himself in his own store that he forgot the details—generating new clients, paying taxes, controlling expenses, managing inventory, and all the other dotted I's and crossed T's that make or break a business, big or small.

So, yes; find something that you love to do, and do it. But remember that you are the business first and the client second.

WHEN YOUR PASSION GETS
YOU IN TROUBLE
ACCELERATORS

 What details in your business are you prone to overlook or forget about?

 How would you spend your time if all of the detailed tasks were handled by someone better at doing them than you?

 How can you get these details covered by someone else, so that you can focus on the things you're best at doing?

THE NAME'S BOND ...
JAMES BOND

"An organization's ability to learn, and to translate that learning into action rapidly, is the ultimate competitive advantage."

Jack Welch

You may never have had experience with business and competitive intelligence. Most small and mid-sized companies either do not have the resources for an internal competitive intelligence department, or they farm out those needs to a third party. Regardless, they certainly do not readily advertise they are gathering actionable intelligence on competitors. The process of gathering competitive intelligence is not as James Bond as it sounds. Professionals in this space sift through mountains of open-source data to predict the movements of competitors. Most competitive intelligence deals with strategic competitive trends, but you can take advantage of some of the same open-source data that drives the larger predictive competitive models.

On any level, social media is a boon for intelligence gathering. Follow your competition on all the major social-media platforms. If you are familiar with a competitor's movers and shakers, follow their professional and personal social media feeds if they are publicly accessible. By paying close attention, and sometimes reading between the lines, you can infer quite a bit. For example, if a competitor's main social media feeds are talking about making a big announcement soon and the head of their real-estate department is grousing about working late, your competition might be making a big move. If your competition is dealing to end users, social listening might help you gauge the overall satisfaction of their customer base.

The drawback to performing your own competitive intelligence is that it can be time-consuming, depending on how far down the rabbit hole you wish to take it. If you sneak a peek at your own social media during the day or at lunch, replace that with checking out the competition. Any of this information that is publicly accessible can give you an advantage and assist you in making better decisions about your own business.

THE NAME'S BOND ...
JAMES BOND
ACCELERATORS

 What open sources of competitive intelligence data do you have or can you get access to?

 In what ways can you consistently gather "competitive intelligence" in your market?

 What kind of process can you establish to enable you to keep a finger on the pulse of your industry, market, and/or competitors?

TOUCHSTONES

"I take inspiration from everyone and everything. I'm inspired by current champions, former champions, true competitors, people dedicated to their dream, hard workers, dreamers, believers, achievers."

Connor McGregor

You may have noticed a number of these accelerators take examples or quotes from authors, poets, or other artists. Their inclusion has been intentional. Artists, in any medium, are the personification of creativity within our society. While you may not view a creative business solution in the same category as *Starry Night*, you are drawing from the same well of creativity Vincent van Gogh pitched in his bucket. Do not discount the artistry of business. What Van Gogh did with paint and canvas, you do with vision, business acumen, and a sense of mission.

An artist seeks to express and inspire. A business leader seeks to do the same. Your expression is either the product, service, or innovation that holds your passion or it's the customers for whom you have passion. To translate that unique expression, you must inspire a team to work in concert for a common goal. An artist has an eye for proportion and scope for their works. A business leader must define their venture by the same parameters. Daily, you are a symphony conductor, painter, sculptor, and writer as you create your business narrative.

I have a number of statuettes, symbols, and tchotchkes strategically placed around my office. If you were to visit, you'd likely see them as just décor. Each of them has a specific meaning, for they serve as reminders of the key points that are critical to my success. In most instances, they are reminders of important lessons learned in my life that point the way to a better future.

TOUCHSTONES
ACCELERATORS

✗ Find one or two pieces of art, statuettes, or symbols that inspire you and keep it close to your work area. It may be a song, a painting used as your desktop's background, a quotation written on a sticky note— the medium doesn't matter as long as the meaning, artistry, and inspiration are at hand.

✗ Take some time to "craft the story" around that important symbol that gives it significant meaning.

✗ When you doubt yourself or feel the tedium of paperwork dragging you down, look to your creative touchstone and remind yourself of its meaning. Remember—you are just as much the artist as the person who crafted this important piece.

FEARED THINGS FIRST

"Genius is one percent inspiration and ninety-nine percent perspiration."

Thomas A. Edison

Nothing is worse than when a black hole develops in your mind. A creative exhaustion that sucks even bad ideas into a disparaging singularity that makes you wonder if you'll *ever* hatch another original thought. You've been at this point often enough to know that despair, despondence, and creative meltdown isn't far over the horizon. How do you put the cork in the black hole?

As counterintuitive as this sounds, immediately stop your present project and do something you hate. Balance your checkbook, pay bills, clean out the gutters, get cracking on that pivot table, or whatever activity you loathe doing more than anything else in the world. That sounds like a terrible idea. Why would anyone do something they hate as a cure for stymied inspiration?

Your mind is designed to shield you from unpleasantness. When you are in the midst of something you can't possibly stand to do, your thoughts will wander to more enjoyable endeavors. Unless your focus is strong enough to resist playing the "I'd rather be doing x, y, or z" game, your attention will invariably fall upon the things you love to do. Suddenly, that black-hole cork you desperately tried to find earlier will come wafting to the forefront of your creative process.

While this method might sound like a Jedi mind trick, you're leveraging your brain's defenses to your benefit. Everyone's mind works differently, so this might not work for you. However, there is some trigger that snaps you out of the doldrums. The next time you have an "A-ha!" moment, take a minute to note what was happening around you when brilliance struck. Were you cooking? Was there a song on the radio? Cataloging these stimuli will help you understand your unique creative processes for the next time you can't think of a single thing.

FEARED THINGS FIRST

ACCELERATORS

 When was your last "A-ha!" moment?

 What were you doing immediately before this moment?

 Take a moment to identify a few of your "least favorite things" that require your attention.

 Start every day doing the feared thing first, but keep an inspiration notepad close at hand.

52

THE RUDDER AND THE ASTROLABE

"A mission statement is not something you write overnight. But fundamentally, your mission statement becomes your constitution, the solid expression of your vision and values. It becomes the criterion by which you measure everything else in your life."

Stephen Covey

Proverbs 29:18 (KJV): "Where there is no vision, the people perish: but he that keepeth the law, happy is he." That verse has always been a favorite of mine and touches on every point discussed within this text. One other translation reads, "Where there is no vision, the people cast off restraint." Can you see the visual of an entire group of people "casting off restraint"? That literally means they run around aimlessly (like chickens with their heads cut off).

As an entrepreneur, innovator, or change agent, the two constants that connect every aspect of business are vision and values (the law). Both intangibles are the North Star we use to guide our respective ships. Like a rudder and astrolabe, vision and values must be perfectly aligned for us to reach our destination. There are no shortcuts where either vision or values are concerned, unless we risk taking our ship too close to rocky shoals.

Maintaining both vision and values is never an easy task. We often act as though the words "easy" and "happy" are synonymous—they are not. There always are, and will always be, easy temptations that may be difficult to shy away from. Fudging mileage or depreciation might reduce your taxable income, but what happens when you get audited? Giving into those temptations will only bring you worry and guilt. Of course, the Book of Proverbs reference to happiness has to do with keeping God's law, which is the ultimate basis for a strong sense of values—ethical behavior. Both in business and your personal life, living according to a set of values results in a security that brings lasting happiness every single time. Doing the right thing is often difficult. As an entrepreneur, innovator, and change agent, you often have the freedom to do what you want; however, as the saying goes, the true freedom comes in doing what we ought.

Have faith, persevere, and grow from your mistakes. If you take nothing else from this text, those three points will see you through any storm. Good fortunes, and God bless.

THE RUDDER AND THE ASTROLABE

ACCELERATORS

 Where do you see yourself, your business, or your organization in the next five years? What things will you have achieved or accomplished? What will you look like? How will you feel?

 What are the core values or beliefs you have about your life, business or organization?

 Now build a twelve-month plan to get you at least twenty percent of the way to your five-year vision, but one that operates within the boundaries of your core values.

AN EXCERPT FROM
JEFF STANDRIDGE'S
GOLD STANDARD

"Leadership is lifting a person's vision to high sights, the raising of a person's performance to a higher standard, the building of a personality beyond its normal limitations."

Peter Drucker

THINK FORWARD
AND INNOVATE

Those who achieve much in life don't do so by accident. Successful people harness the power of positive, proactive thinking using mental clarity. They develop a laser-focused vision of their aspirations, and they cultivate a burning desire for its achievement. This programming, or reprogramming, as the case may be, of our subconscious minds can best be accomplished by having a crystal-clear vision of our desired future, one that is driven by this future state orientation.

Before you think I've lost my mind, before you think that I'm trying to sell you some kind of hocus-pocus mumbo-jumbo or "manifestation snake oil," let me just say this: I have seen this work in my own life and in the lives of other individuals and organizations for years. I will acknowledge that countless "success gurus" merely extol the virtues of visualization as a means of achievement. "Simply visualize in your mind what you want, and it will manifest," they say. While I am in agreement with the power of visualization, in my experience, the real power comes in having absolute and detailed mental clarity about your aspirations and destinations. The act of visualization by itself is never enough to succeed. Once we get absolute clarity on a goal, an aspiration, or a destination, and we fix that achievement in our mind, we tend to focus on it repeatedly. That continued positive reinforcement on the desired outcome plants itself deep in our subconscious, resulting in physical changes within our conscious mind. Like the heat-seeking missile described earlier, we become acutely aware of opportunities we would have simply passed over before, because of this mental clarity. This results in physical changes within our bodies, and we begin to act and behave differently. This acknowledgment of these previously unrecognized opportunities, combined with a set of new behaviors that move us rapidly toward the object/destination of our desire, produces positive outcomes at a rate that can at times appear to be nothing short of miraculous. This powerful concept that represents the **third reality** of Gold Standard Leadership:

> "Successful leaders have
> a future orientation."

It's been said before that "if you don't know where we're going, any road will take you there." At the end of the previous chapter, you were instructed to write out, in vivid detail and in the present tense, precisely what you wanted your ideal life to look like in the future. While this process can be difficult if you've never attempted it, the end result is a line you've drawn in the sands of the subconscious that creates a concrete "reality" that your conscious mind and your body conspire to create.

This process is not unlike the thermostat in your home. When you set an objective at some point in the future, it acts as the temperature setting on your thermostat. For instance, let's say you set the thermostat in your home to seventy degrees during the winter. However, one of your kids leaves the front door open, and a blast of cold wind enters the home and drops the temperature to sixty-seven degrees.

Automatically and without effort, the thermostat "clicks." The flames of the gas burner are kicked on, power is sent to the fan motors, and the machinery begins to whirl. The heated air forces its way through the cold air lining the ductwork, up through the vents, and into a house systematically raising the temperature back to the "goal" level. This process works similarly to the "auto-regulator" or "thermostat" that sits in our subconscious minds.

Put another way, successful people know where they are going and they permanently "fix" the thermostats of their subconscious minds to take them there. They may not initially understand the finer points of how to get there, but they know precisely where they are going. That vision is infectious and helps cast the vision to those around them as well. When you are a leader focused on the future, you empower yourself to practice asymmetrical thinking that builds the trust and ever-essential confidence of your team. If you don't have the power to look further than what is just sitting in front of you, how can you expect to be an effective leader?

In addition to envisioning the future as you see it, the best of the best know how to accelerate arrival at their intended destination. This concept can be leveraged in personal situations, within small teams, or across large organizations. I call it "Peak Performance Planning, " and it looks something like this:

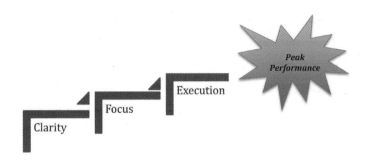

Peak Performance Planning

Before we can make sustained, much less accelerated, progress toward the achievement of our goals and objectives, we must have absolute clarity as to what we want to achieve in the first place. If we are leading a team of people, the entire team must share in that same level of clarity. It is only after we develop absolute clarity that we can begin to cultivate a focused attention on its achievement. Focused attention leads us to develop specific and detailed action plans that enable an efficient execution. Absent are the wasted efforts of false starts, unforeseen detours, or distractions of bright, shiny objects that kill so many good intentions. The simple concept of focus has been one that I have leveraged to success in both my personal and professional life. How we spend our time is vital to Peak Performance—or the accelerated achievement of our desires. Without clarity of purpose, we are prone to rushing headlong down frustrating and failure-riddled rabbit trails. Successful leaders take advantage of this concept of "Peak Performance Planning," by addressing each component individually and sequentially.

Absolute Clarity

One key aspect of achieving absolute clarity is developing a keen understanding of mission, vision, and values. In an organizational setting, this is commonly referred to as "strategic planning." It has been my experience that most strategic plans are an attempt to capture a snapshot of everything that is currently being done in an organization. The exercise is presented so no one feels alienated or gets their feelings hurt by not being "in the know." Missing from the strategic plan is how to achieve absolute clarity of the future direction of the organization. I challenge this predisposition at every opportunity! The strategic plans that we help companies, institutions, organizations, and individual creativity are clear, concise, and targeted. Plans of this nature usually consist of no more than three to five pages that can be used as a roadmap to the intended destination over the next three to five to ten years.

The process of refining and/or developing absolute clarity around mission, vision, and values can be carried out with individuals, groups, teams, or companies. A common obstacle exists in unclear, or at least inconsistent, definitions of what mission, vision, and values mean.

The **mission** of an individual or group is simply why it exists or why it was created. Every organization has a mission, and virtually everything else flows from this sense of mission. Having a deep understanding of mission allows an organization to ensure that its current/future plans of action are in alignment and absent of distraction or wasted effort.

It is my belief that individuals also have a unique mission, or "calling." Each of us was created to fulfill a unique role, and understanding that role fuels our passion and helps us experience a sense of fulfillment when we act in alignment with that calling. I often explain that for some people, their vocation is their calling. Many physicians, nurses, teachers, pastors, counselors, and a host of others have an internal pull toward their chosen profession. These professionals get up every day and go to work as a normal part of their putting food on the table. The difference between these those who "just have a job" and the "called" is a matter of alignment. The called feed their souls with their professions as their vocation *supports* their calling. Fulfillment of their calling requires money and their vocation supplies funding to fulfill that calling. Perhaps their calling requires access to large numbers of people, and their chosen vocation, job, or profession provides access to these people.

There is a host of other ways in which their vocation supports them and the fulfillment of their calling, but the important point is that they have discovered their calling and are acting in alignment with that calling.

I have taught my daughters about discovering their calling from the time they were old enough to understand the concept. When speaking with my daughters, I frequently used this borrowed phrase: "Figure out what your calling is, then find a way to get paid for it, and you'll never have to work a day in your life." At the center point of our souls, we yearn to be significant. We have a deep desire and are drawn to fulfill our calling. When we build the fulfillment of our calling into our everyday lives and ascertain the connection between our vocations and our calling, our normal course of action is in alignment with what we feel we should be doing. When we know why we exist, and we operate in a manner consistent with this understanding, we experience a sense of fulfillment that keeps us satisfied and motivated. Additionally, the alignment between mind, soul, and body creates the uncommon ability to persevere in the face of adversity.

Successful leaders and top performers are mission-oriented people. They have an inherent understanding of their own personal calling. They lead their organizations to develop that same profound understanding of their corporate mission. Once they have that understanding, they ensure that their plans and actions are in alignment with that mission. It is this deep sense of mission that enables successful leaders and top performers to cast a compelling future vision. Armed with that vision, they do just that—create the future they have envisioned.

While mission has to do with purpose or calling, the **vision** of an individual or group has to do with a specific destination or point in the future. Simply put, successful leaders and top performers know precisely where they are going. They look out three, five, seven, or ten years down the road and define with crystal clarity what their intended future will look like at that time. They describe in objective and measurable terms the accomplishments they intend to achieve, the circumstances that will be created, and/or the results they plan to deliver.

The mission, purpose, or calling of an individual or group is fairly static and consistent over time. Seldom, without undergoing a fairly extensive personal transformation, does one's life purpose or calling change. We usually have a single mission or purpose throughout our lifetime—we are who we are. The same trend applies to groups or organizations—we've always done business this way and that way it will stay. These statements, of course, are a generalization but the comfort of stagnation is a universal constant.

Mission, purpose, and calling are all tied to predefined points in the future. Vision, on the other hand, tends to change over time. As we go about fulfilling our respective missions, the destination at which we expect to arrive in this five-year period will be different in a succeeding five-year period. This is referred to as progress. Over a fifteen-year period, our mission may not have changed a bit. Forward progress suggests that we will be at a far different place and perhaps a series of destinations along the way than when we started many years previously.

Values, or "core values," as they are sometimes called, establish guardrails for the environment we create in executing our mission and/or pursue our intended vision. Values include the things that are important to us as we build and grow our businesses. They help employees *understand how* to go about their jobs, as they help the company fulfill its mission and realize its vision. Values like customer service, quality, teamwork, and integrity often make the list of core values for a company.

The next step in the process of achieving clarity involves precisely articulating, in a measurable way, the goals, results, or outcomes we are seeking to achieve. These goals, results, or outcomes must be so vibrant that the assessment of their achievement is a simple yes or no answer. If the achievement of the goal cannot be measured, or a question about its attainment cannot be answered with a yes/no answer, the goal is not specific or precise enough. In a personal situation, absolute clarity usually involves a specific deadline or target date, as well as the tangible goal, result, or outcome. In a team or organizational structure, the absolute clarity is the same with the addition of identifying individuals or groups who are responsible for their portion of the overall achievement.

"No guessing" is the mantra when it comes to gaining clarity within organizations. What's going to be done, by when, and by whom are three vital questions that must be answered at all costs. Knowing the answers to these questions, having them written down and easily accessible and then reviewing them frequently often means the difference between success and failure. This statement of clarity, with all of its pieces, is the first step in the Peak Performance Planning Process. Eliminate or overlook it at your peril.

Focused Attention

Once we have absolute clarity on our mission, vision, values, and the desired goals, outcomes, or results we are seeking to achieve, we can begin to establish a focused attention on their attainment. Focused attention involves a regular review of the desired state (the ideal state), the assessment of where we stand relative to that desired state (the currently achieved state), and understanding the difference between the two (the gap).

At this point, practicing visualization becomes useful. Regularly reviewing the statement of clarity that was crafted above, and taking a moment to visualize that desired state on a frequent basis creates a dissonance between where we are and where we want to be. That discord between the two states is a constant reminder that we are out of alignment with our desired future. It is this sense of misalignment that spurs us to close this gap to achieve congruence.

I first learned the power behind the principle of focused attention when I was a senior in college. I worked full-time throughout college as an emergency medical technician (EMT) for a hospital-based paramedic ambulance service. Based on my experience there, I decided to change my major to respiratory therapy for one single reason—I wanted to become a medical flight crewmember for the Angel Flight Transport Team (Angel One) at Arkansas Children's Hospital. I had interacted with the various helicopter teams that had flown to our small community hospital to pick up patients. I also knew that the Angel One crew consisted of a Registered Nurse and a respiratory therapist/EMT. When the helicopter circled our facility before landing on our rooftop helipad, I was awestruck. I had admired the flight suits, the near rock star status they enjoyed as they became the heroes of whatever malady was occurring at the time. It didn't require many interactions before I was figuring out the academic path required to change my major and become one of those crew members.

At that time, the professional portion of the respiratory-therapy curriculum was thirteen months, beginning the first of June one year and finishing the end of June the following year. Knowing that I had to continue working full-time to meet my financial obligations, on the first day of the respiratory-therapy program, I set up an interview for an entry-level position at both University Hospital and at Arkansas Children's Hospital. Due to my emergency-room and ambulance experience, University Hospital promptly offered me a job. I shared with them that I had another interview, and I would let them know my answer soon.

When I waltzed into the interview at Arkansas Children's Hospital a couple of hours later, I declared to my interviewer, "I've just begun the respiratory-therapy program. In thirteen months, I'm going to graduate and come fly on your helicopter. Now, if you would like to go ahead and hire me, you'll have plenty of time to train me before I graduate."

My interviewer politely informed me that while they might have a position open filling oxygen tanks. The members of the flight team were analogous to the military's special operation groups, and one usually had years of experience before being considered for a role.

I responded, "Well, I'm not interested in an 'oxygen tech' position, so I'm going to work at University Hospital. Here's my phone number, when you change your mind, please give me a call." Note that I didn't even say *"if"* you change your mind. I said *"when."*

Fast-forward about six months, and I happened to be doing clinical rotations at Arkansas Children's Hospital. On the last day of clinical in early December, I received a note that the director of the department wanted to see me. This was the same director with whom I had interviewed on the first day of the program. She informed me that they had been monitoring my performance during my clinical and she was pleased to offer me a full-time position in the department. Excitedly, I immediately inquired, "On the helicopter team?"

Disappointed at her answer, I learned that I would be working first in the non-critical-care areas. She assured me that as I gained experience, I would have the opportunity to rotate through the emergency room, the pediatric ICU, the neonatal ICU, and other units. I quickly accepted and gave my two-weeks notice at University Hospital.

Fast-forward to the end of April, and I received word once again that the Director wanted to see me. I will never forget the moment I walked into her office. She was sitting there with the head of the Flight Team. They informed me that my performance had been outstanding and they had an opening on the Flight Team. Rather than opening up the position to interview, they wanted to slot me on the team. A two-month orientation period was required, which coincided precisely with my graduation in June. Almost thirty years later, I remember what I did as I walked out of that office. I jumped in the air and kicked my heels together. If I listen to my memories closely enough, I can still hear them laughing at me as I walked down the hall.

My orientation lasted the planned two months. Coincidentally the day following graduation, I received my "wings" and worked my first shift as a fully recognized member of the Angel One Flight Team. It was a dream come true. More importantly, my wings represented tangible evidence that "successful people have a future orientation" early in my life. I had "visioned" my way into a career direction that would not only change my life, but it would also be the start of a new life. A cute young RN began her orientation as a Flight Nurse as my orientation period ended. That cute young RN has been my wife of nearly three decades and the mother of my beautiful, now grown, daughters.

Consistent Execution

Once we have absolute clarity, followed by a focused attention on the achievement of that which we desire, it is time to build a detailed plan of execution. What specifically must we do consistently and what action steps do we need to make are fundamental questions for achieving that which we have outlined in our statement of clarity. The answers to these questions should be as specific as possible. Fleshing out all of the key actions that must be taken closes the gap between the desired state and the current state. Here are a few pointers to keep you on track:

⚡ BE SPECIFIC AND SET MEASURABLE GOALS

When you are specific and reasonable, you increase your success rate. Being able to measure your goals is very important because if you can't see what you are working towards you'll likely end up off-track … and fast.

⚡ BREAK YOUR GOALS INTO SMALLER TASKS

Big goals can be overwhelming. When you break bigger goals down into smaller ones you dramatically increase the likelihood of success.

∦ CREATE SCHEDULE LISTS

Make your list and check it twice. When you create lists and schedules, you hold yourself accountable to take action and get it done.

∦ UTILIZE TIMELINES

It's been said that goals without timelines are simply wishes. Enough said…

When you take the time to write down your blueprint to success, you open the door to ensuring you reach your goals quickly and efficiently. Leaders often run astray thinking that success is automatic or past glories translate to future wins. All too often those mentalities fail miserably. However, when leaders finally figure out that a humble, yet palpable, plan of action can make all the difference, they wonder why it took them so long to put pen to paper.

A Bias for Action

In any field, whenever you want to achieve something, you must define your desired results, goals, and/or aspirations. More important than the definition, you must *take action*. It's been said that it is not enough to stare up the steps; we must also step up the stairs. A clear understanding of what you want is inexorably linked to the actions you must take to achieve it.

For people to jump on your bandwagon, they need to see the vision to which you aspire, and they need to feel confident in the path to get there. I've heard it said that "it's not enough to stare up the steps, you must also step up the stairs." Leaders have the responsibility for creating this sense of clarity and for making sustained action possible.

Obviously, there will be hurdles to clear on your journey, but having a strong sense of mission and that mission will help you clear those hurdles. Perseverance is bred by knowing who you are (your calling or mission) and where you're going (your vision). The challenges you face will test your commitment to that mission and vision. Successful leaders know that abandoning a cause isn't an option. They embrace the importance of the vision, and other people are attracted do that commitment. This sense of clarity, passion, and commitment attracts committed followers and propels us toward success in any endeavor.

MINI-ACCELERATORS

John Quincy Adams—"If your actions inspire others to dream more, learn more, do more, and become more, you are a leader."

African proverb—"An army of sheep led by a lion can beat an army of lions led by a sheep."

Klaus Balkenhol—"There is a difference between being a leader and being a boss. Both are based on authority. A boss demands blind obedience; a leader earns his authority through understanding and trust."

Ken Blanchard—"The greatest leaders mobilize others by coalescing people around a shared vision."

Napoleon Bonaparte—"A leader is a dealer in hope."

Bill Bradley—"Leadership is unlocking people's potential to become better."

Rosalynn Carter—"A leader takes people where they want to go. A great leader takes people where they don't necessarily want to go, but ought to be."

Stephen Covey—"What you do has far greater impact than what you say."

Max DePree—"The first responsibility of a leader is to define reality. The last is to say thank you. In between, the leader is a servant."

Peter Drucker—"Leadership is lifting a person's vision to high sights, the raising of a person's performance to a higher standard, the building of a personality beyond its normal limitations."

Dwight Eisenhower—"The supreme quality of leadership is integrity."

King George VI—"The highest of distinctions is service to others."

Pete Hoekstra—"Real leadership is leaders recognizing that they serve the people that they lead."

Eric Hoffer—"The leader has to be practical and a realist, yet must talk the language of the visionary and the idealist."

Michael Jordan—"Earn your leadership every day."

John F. Kennedy—"Leadership and learning are indispensable to one another."

Abraham Lincoln—"Give me six hours to chop down a tree and I will spend the first four sharpening the axe."

General James "Chaos" Mattis—"I don't lose any sleep at night over the potential for failure. I cannot even spell the word."

Ralph Moody—"Always remember, Son, the best boss is the one who bosses the least. Whether it's cattle, or horses, or men; the least government is the best government."

General George S. Patton—"If everybody is thinking alike, then somebody isn't thinking."

Ross Perot—"Lead and inspire people. Don't try to manage and manipulate people. Inventories can be managed but people must be lead."

General John J. Pershing—"A competent leader can get efficient service from poor troops, while on the contrary an incapable leader can demoralize the best of troops."

Polybius—"A good general not only sees the way to victory; he also knows when victory is impossible."

General Colin Powell—"Being responsible sometimes means pissing people off."

Beth Revis—"A leader isn't someone who forces others to make him stronger; a leader is someone willing to give his strength to others so that they may have the strength to stand on their own."

Eleanor Roosevelt—"To handle yourself, use your head; to handle others, use your heart."

General Norman Schwarzkopf—"Leadership is a potent combination of strategy and character. But if you must be without one, be without the strategy."

Albert Schweitzer—"Example is not the main thing in influencing others. It is the only thing."

Adlai E. Stevenson II—"It's hard to lead a cavalry charge if you think you look funny on a horse."

Robert Louis Stevenson—"Keep your fears to yourself, but share your courage with others."

Unknown—"My responsibility is getting all my players playing for the name on the front of the jersey, not the one on the back."

Margaret Thatcher—"Do you know that one of the great problems of our age is that we are governed by people who care more about feelings than they do about thoughts and ideas?"

Robert Townsend—"A leader is not an administrator who loves to run others, but someone who carries water for his people so that they can get on with their jobs."

Brian Tracy—"Leaders think and talk about the solutions. Followers think and talk about the problems."

William Arthur Ward—"The mediocre teacher tells. The good teacher explains. The superior teacher demonstrates. The great teacher inspires."

Woodrow Wilson—"Leadership does not always wear the harness of compromise."

Fuchan Yuan—"There are three essentials to leadership: humility, clarity and courage."

ABOUT DR. JEFF D. STANDRIDGE

Dr. Jeff Standridge helps organizations and their leaders generate sustained results in the areas of innovation, strategy, profit growth, organizational effectiveness, and leadership. Formerly a Vice President for Acxiom Corporation, he has led established and startup business units in North and South America, Europe, Asia and the Middle East.

Jeff now serves as Chief Catalyst for the Conductor (www.ARConductor.org), is Co-founder of Cadron Capital Partners and Jeff Standridge Innovation Partners, and teaches Entrepreneurial Finance at the University of Central Arkansas (www.UCA.edu).

He has been an invited speaker, trainer, and/or consultant for numerous businesses, organizations, and institutions of higher education around the world. In addition to his executive coaching and custom-tailored consulting, he has received accolades for his World Class presentations, training programs and workshops, including:

- **Corporate Innovation Accelerator**—for companies of all sizes, across all industries who want to drive more innovative thinking and problem-solving

- **Faculty Innovation Accelerator**—for academic institutions of all types who are looking to drive more innovative research and problem-solving

- **The Commercialization Accelerator**—for research institutions wanting to create an increased focus on commercializing their research

- **Sales Acceleration Workshop**—for companies that want to build a high-performance sales engine

- **Success Secrets of World-Class Leaders**—for organizations of all kinds that want to build their leadership bench and empower their leaders for greater success

- **Coaching for World-Class Performance**—for companies that want to create a culture of world-class performance and world-class teamwork.

Jeff and his wife, Lori, make their home in Conway, Arkansas.

To learn more about Dr. Standridge or Jeff Standridge Innovation Partners, visit his website at JeffStandridge.com.

Reader's Guide

Topic: Chapter Number